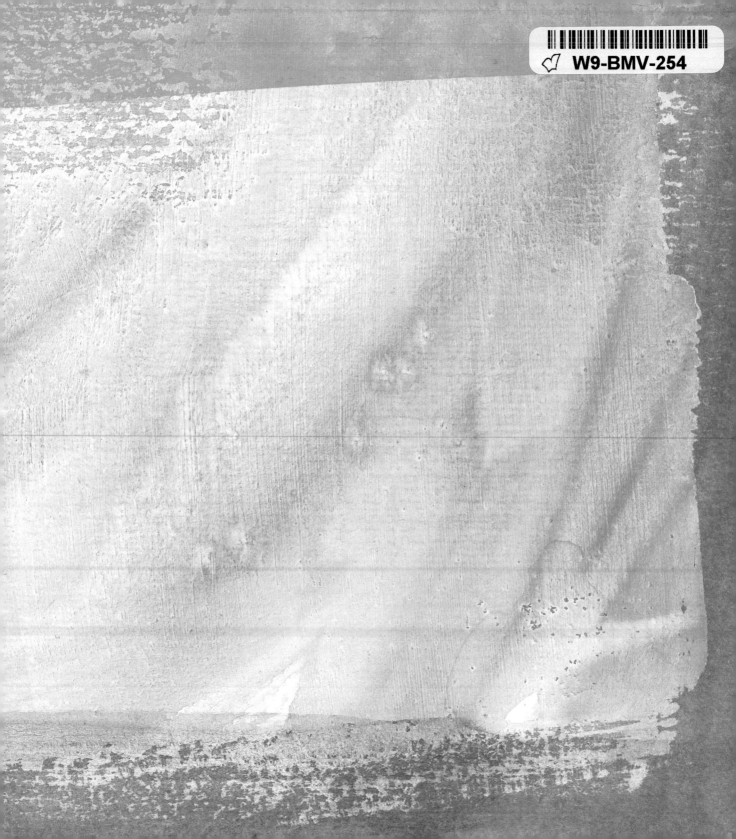

THE BOOK OF
Wizard Parties

In Which the Wizard Shares the Secrets of Creating Enchanted Gatherings

Illustrated by Marla Baggetta

LARK BOOKS

A Division of Sterling Publishing Company, Inc.

NEW YORK

AUTHORS
Janice Eaton Kilby
Terry Taylor

**ART DIRECTION, DESIGN &
BACKGROUND ILLUSTRATIONS**
Susan McBride

**COVER, SPOT &
CHAPTER ILLUSTRATIONS**
Marla Baggetta

TECHNICAL ILLUSTRATIONS
Orrin Lundgren

ASSISTANT EDITOR
Veronika Alice Gunter
EDITORIAL ASSISTANT
Rain Newcomb
EDITORIAL INTERN:
Anne Wolff Hollyfield

ASSISTANT ART DIRECTOR
Hannes Charen
ART INTERNS:
Barbara Murray
Amanda Robbins
Shannon Yokeley

Library of Congress Cataloging-in-Publication Data Available

10 9 8 7 6 5 4 3 2 1

First Edition

Published by Lark Books, a division of
Sterling Publishing Co., Inc.
387 Park Avenue South, New York, N.Y. 10016

© 2002, Lark Books
Illustrations © 2002, Marla Baggetta

Distributed in Canada by Sterling Publishing,
c/o Canadian Manda Group, One Atlantic Ave., Suite 105
Toronto, Ontario, Canada M6K 3E7

Distributed in the U.K. by:
Guild of Master Craftsman Publications Ltd.
Castle Place
166 High Street
Lewes
East Sussex
England
BN7 1XU
Tel: (+ 44) 1273 477374
Fax: (+ 44) 1273 478606
Email: pubs@thegmcgroup.com
Web: www.gmcpublications.com

Distributed in Australia by Capricorn Link (Australia) Pty Ltd., P.O. Box 704, Windsor, NSW 2756
Australia

If you have questions or comments about this book, please contact:
Lark Books
67 Broadway
Asheville, NC 28801
(828) 236-9730

Printed in China

ISBN 1-57990-292-8

Acknowledgments

It's an Aha! moment to discover how many wizards surround you when you really need them. Thank you to my brilliant collaborators Terry Taylor and Susan McBride and my other gifted colleagues at Lark—especially the elves among the Assistant Editors—for their enthusiastic help and home-cooked meals. As always, enduring love and thanks to Tip, Ryan, and Angela Kilby, the people who helped me start it all—and to Marjorie Morgan Koman, who carted me to the public library all those many Saturdays long ago.

J.E.K.

Our inspirational angels appear in many guises and in unexpected places. I wish I had thanked Mrs. Lucille Rector, one of my seventh-grade teachers, for lessons in huck embroidery, weaving rush seats, ceramics, and—my personal favorites—crafting dioramas and bulletin boards, just a few of the things she taught that weren't even mentioned in our science and health textbooks. Mrs. Rector, I thank you now. May every seventh-grader be so inspired.

T.T.

It is a privilege to work on books for children, especially in the company of Wizards, familiars and fairies. A special thank you to Marla Baggetta and Orrin Lundgren.

S.M.

TABLE of

CONTENTS

INTRODUCTION

by the Wizard

After Lark Books published my *Book of Wizard Craft* last year, I thought I'd take a nice, long vacation. I'd already spent 600 years working on that book, for goodness' sake! Ever since I was a young wizard, I've kept notes on how to make useful things for wizard work. I also wrote down many of the stories wizards tell each other late at night. I shared some of my own adventures too.

But it wasn't easy to fit 600 years into only one book. I had several dozen more chests of notes, drawings, and keepsakes hidden in a secret cave guarded by dwarves. But when I told my editors about them, they threw up their hands and said we'd have to wait for the next book!

SO HERE IT IS.

How to Use
THIS BOOK

This new book of mine is all about wizard parties, how young wizards can have fun together and celebrate special times. My best memories are the times I spent with my friends at their castles or mine, playing games and making magic. Like the time I sent 500 mice to sing for Merlin at his 500th birthday party at King Arthur's court. Or the holiday party when my dragon friends blasted "Welcome!" in green and red smoke over my front door.

This book tells how to make everything you need for special theme parties and for parties for each season (spring, summer, fall, and winter). I include instructions for decorations, special partywear, party favors, crafts, games, and stories you can read aloud. Mix potions for an Alchemists' Gathering. Make a Throne of the Realm for a Merlin's Birthday Parley. Build a Merry Maypole for a Welcome Springtime Fairy Frolic. You can even make it "snow" inside for a Wizard's Winter Revels!

Follow the directions in my chapter on Basic Wizard's Gear (page 135) to make easy party robes, hats, and other items. Or make special party clothes, including a Chinese Wizard's Robe. Make Fairy Wands and Wings, or a Crystal Crown (just like Glinda the Good Witch wore when I met her in the Land of Oz long ago).

It's very wizardly to make things with your own hands! You and your party guests will have fun making easy craft projects they can take home later. Or make some party favors ahead of time. Learn to play my favorite party games, too. How about Dragon Wrestling, Cabbage Bowling, Tea Leaf Reading, or Egyptian Dice?

My directions for each party include special food and drink recipes such as Mandrake Cupcakes and Lavender Lemonade. Some of them I invented myself, and some I got from other wizards. The trooping fairies (who spend all their time feasting outdoors) gave me tips, too. I've updated the recipes for modern cooks, because most of us just don't have time to roast a whole ox these days.

You'll also find a special story for every party in this book. You (or a friendly adult wizard) can read it aloud to your guests. If you have a Spirited Druid Halloween Gathering, I dare you to turn out the lights and read the tale of the Beheading Ball. Or hear Merlin's story about what really happened to King Arthur and the Sword in the Stone. I share legends and stories from my own past too, including tales about famous alchemists and dragons.

Use this book however you wish! Follow my directions to give the party of your choice. Or mix and match different activities to invent a party of your own. (Several of my sister witches told me they're giving a Good Witch and Goddess Party. They're making Goddess of Beauty robes on page 109, and Fairy Wands on page 83. I was glad to hear that.)

I also include guides on how to pronounce some wizardly words and names (in case you haven't learned them yet). One caution: If you see the snake symbol next to a how-to project, you must find an adult wizard or nonwizard to help you. I mean it, I'm serious! If you ignore me, I'll turn you into a Giant Slug and you'll be late for everything, including dinner.

ADULT WIZARD SUPERVISION!

NOW, FOR MY BEST PARTY SECRETS...

SOME THOUGHTS ON
Party Giving & Going

If you want to be a well-mannered wizard, pay attention. When you give a party, invite guests at least two or three weeks before the event. That way, your friends can get their party robes ready and look forward to your party. You can invite people by telephone, but I think it's much nicer to send written invitations in the mail. (See the next page, on how to make party invitations.) Then you can call anyone who didn't understand the R.S.V.P. on your invitation (more below on that subject).

If you're invited to a party, telephone the host or hostess right away to tell them if you can come. (That's why you'll see the letters, "RSVP" on an invitation. They stand for some long French words that mean, "Call me up, or you are an ill-mannered troll!") Don't depend on your host being able to read your mind. His skills as a wizard may not be that strong yet. And don't ever just show up the day of the party without calling. Your host needs to know how many people are coming. That way, his kitchen dragon will know how many cookies to roast.

What happens if you're invited to a party given by someone you don't know well? Or you're not sure you like that person? Well, a real wizard would say "Yes" to the invitation. Go, be a good guest, and see what happens. At least you won't spend the day alone in your room. Maybe you'll make some new friends!

On the other hand, what if you hear about a party you weren't invited to? My advice is to start making plans to give your own party. Don't wait for other people to make fun, start making your own! You'll be surprised by how many friends you attract. Make the first move to have people over to your cavern or castle. You'll be on their guest lists in the future. Be patient, however. I once invited Sir O'Blihveehuss to a party. He was a very grand Irish wizard, and I didn't know him very well. He seemed to have a good time, but he didn't ask me to his castle—until 200 years had passed! It turned out he gave regular parties, but only every couple of centuries. His house elf didn't have to dust much that way.

When you give a party, help your guests enjoy themselves. Break the ice and help strangers meet each other. If any guests seem shy, spend some extra time with them. Ask them to help you, or try to match them up with other guests they can talk to.

If you're a guest, bring a little surprise for your host or hostess with you, perhaps a flower or a small bottle of potion. (If it's a birthday party, gifts are usually, ahem, welcome.) Does your host have a trained, eight-armed, Giant Octopus helping in the kitchen? If not, ask if you can lend a hand. Don't forget to say please, and when it's time to leave, thank whoever invited you. Here's a hint: If you really want to impress your host and the adult wizards in the house, send a thank-you note or call the next day to tell them what a lovely time you had. If you want to be invited to their next party, I have *never* known this to fail!

So go ahead, take this book and start planning how to make magic with your friends. And if you happen to see a silver-haired stranger in a purple cloak at your party, don't worry. Just offer me—er, I mean him—a glass of punch. We wizards never say no to having a good time.

YOU'RE INVITED!

How to Make Fantastic Invitations

The best parties always start with those two magic words: You're invited! My wizard friends and I always tried to top each other's invitations. Can you imagine glowing hieroglyphs (HIGH-row-gliffs) on your front door? Swirls of genie smoke writing messages in the air? Or a mysterious silver envelope in your mailbox, addressed just to you? Looking forward to a party always adds to the fun.

Make invitations that give your guests a hint of things to come. It should shout, "This is not a plain, old party!" Write addresses in golden ink. Send see-through fairy wings or glittering dragon scales. No one will forget to come, that's for sure!

It's easy to make invitations. First, go to the stationery department of a store and buy some envelopes. Choose a size, shape, and color you like. It's easier to buy the envelopes and make the invitation to fit than the other way around (unless you cheat with Shrink-Me- or Expand-O-Spells). At the same time, buy some special paper to make the invitations. Try folding one sheet of paper different ways, and make sure it fits the envelope. Remember which fold you liked the best.

Now for the most important part—the words. A good invitation tells *who*, *what*, *when*, and *where*.

Who is giving the party? (You, Merlin the wizard, or King Tut of Egypt?)
What kind of party is it? (An Alchemists' Gathering or an Aladdin's Cave Party?)
When is it, what date and time? (Your birthday or nightfall on Halloween?)
Where is it? (Your street address or under the biggest tree in your local enchanted grove?)

Add your telephone number, too, so other wizards can call you to say, "Count me in! I'm coming."

Do you have the time to put a Speaking Spell on each invitation? If not, take one blank sheet of white paper (it should be the same size as the special paper you chose for the actual invitations). Write out the invitation by hand, or use a rubber stamp, typewriter, or computer to print it. Check the spelling, date and time, address, and phone number. All correct?

Now add some more magic! This book of mine is chock-full of wizardly designs for every party. Photocopy the ones you like. Cut them out, and glue them to the written invitation. Almost done.

Photocopy the invitation onto the special paper. Add color, glitter, or other decorations if you wish. Let dry, then fold the invitations and stick them in envelopes (don't forget the stamp). Mail them. Now wait for the responses to come flying in!

ALCHEMISTS' GATHERING

In my youth, alchemists gave the most exciting parties. You never knew when something would suddenly explode! Today's young wizards will enjoy safely mixing up some magic at an Alchemists' Gathering. Here are my recipes for potions that bubble and sparkle and spew. Guests will also have fun making Portable Cauldrons and Alchemist's Gold.

Alchemist's Laboratory

HANDY TOOLS for EVERY HOME LABORATORY

- small mixing bowls
- measuring cup for liquids
- measuring spoons
- kitchen spoon
- clean glass jars and bottles with screw-on lids or cork stoppers
- knife
- saucepan
- strainer or coffee filters
- funnel
- eyedropper
- small, clear plastic drinking glasses
- marking pens
- food storage bags
- blow-dryer
- rubber bands
- clear, flexible PVC tubing

Every alchemist (ALL-kem-isst) has a laboratory, and you'll want to create one for your party. Old books show alchemists' labs full of strange-looking jars of bubbling who-knows-what. Impress your guests with a lab stocked with everything you need to make the Fun Recipes for Young Alchemists (page 20).

Set up a special lab area in the party room or kitchen. Lay a piece of plastic sheeting on the work surface and floor. Hang a large cardboard sign that reads, "Caution! Alchemists at Work" or "Danger! Wizard Blasting."

Read the recipe directions and gather what you need. See below for a handy list of tools. True wizards are never wasteful and don't throw many things away. The recycling bins in your home probably have useful items for your lab. Collect glass jars and plastic bottles with lids, pieces of hose or plastic piping, and cardboard. Make sure they're clean. Photocopy the label, write the name of the ingredient on it, and glue or tape it to any box, bag, or bottle you use. You don't want to pick up Wurm Slime when you meant to use Dragon's Blood!

Mix food coloring and water in bottles or jars, and give them labels like Gnome Spew or Toad Sweat. Ask an adult to punch a hole in the top of some of the jar lids and run lengths of clear, plastic tubing from one jar to another. Run a length of tubing into just one jar, and blow bubbles just for fun!

Keep paper and pencil handy for keeping notes and a stopwatch to time experiments. One alchemist lost the formula for turning orange rinds into gold, because he forgot to keep notes. He never could eat an orange after that, poor fellow.

PHOTOCOPY THIS LABEL SO YOU'LL KNOW YOUR WURM SLIME FROM YOUR DRAGON'S BLOOD POTION.

Portable Cauldron

Every wizard's lab has a big, three-legged iron pot called a cauldron (CALL-drun). Wizards use them to heat potions (or dinner) over a fire. It isn't easy to move heavy pots from place to place, so modern wizards pack smaller ones when they go wandering. Party guests can make their own mini-cauldrons and take them home to use for breakfast cereal potions.

WHAT YOU NEED

- small plastic or acrylic bowls in bright colors
- large wooden craft beads, small plastic balls, furniture glides, drawer knobs or pulls, corks, or recycled soda bottle caps, 3 per bowl, to serve as legs
- sandpaper
- hot-glue gun and glue sticks
- epoxy adhesive (optional)
- acrylic paint (optional)
- brushes (optional)

INSTRUCTIONS

1. Purchase small bowls. You'll need to know the size of the bowl in order to choose the right legs.

2. Go to the craft or hardware store to buy legs to fit the bowls, or use recycled items.

3. Use the sandpaper to roughen the bottom of each bowl and the tops of the legs, to give the surfaces "tooth" for the glue.

4. Turn the bowls upside down. Glue three, equally spaced legs to the bottom of each bowl. Let the glue dry.

5. For extra cauldron power, use the acrylic paint to decorate bowls with the owners' names, alchemical symbols, or other magical additives.

Dance of the Spheres Centerpiece

ADULT WIZARD SUPERVISION!

Some alchemists tried to explain how the planets and stars moved, and they called the system "the music of the spheres." This simple table centerpiece makes a lively show and doubles as a magic trick.

To impress your fellow party guests, wave your wand over the jar as you sprinkle in the "magic powder" and watch the moth ball spheres dance.

WHAT YOU NEED

• adult wizard
• tall glass vase, large glass jar, or glass bowl
• taper candle
• candle adhesive or modeling clay
• mothballs
• white vinegar
• water
• measuring cup
• magic wand (optional)
• measuring spoon, 1 teaspoon (8 g) size
• magic powder (also known as baking soda)
• matches

INSTRUCTIONS

1. Get an adult wizard to help you. Center the taper inside the vase, and use the candle adhesive or modeling clay to stick it to the bottom.

2. Scatter a handful of the mothballs in the vase.

3. Measure and add ¹/₄ cup (60 mL) of vinegar to the vase.

4. Add the water 1 cup (240 mL) at a time to fill the vase. Don't cover the tip of the candle! Keep count of how many cups you add.

5. While you wave your wand and say, *"Planetas Gaseous!"* (or "Gassy Planets!"), add 1 teaspoon (8 g) of baking soda for each cup of water in the vase. Get an adult wizard to light the candle. The mothballs will start bobbing up, down, and around, and will move for about an hour. When they slow down, add a dash of vinegar and baking soda to start their dance again.

Alchemist's Robe

Like today's scientists, alchemists used symbols for the chemicals in their potions. (That way they didn't have to write out all those long words.) But when you first learn the art of alchemy, it can be hard to remember all of the symbols! An alchemist-in-training can wear this robe in the lab and use it as a handy reminder for what's what. That way, you won't add sulphur to a potion when you meant to add salt! The robe's shorter sleeve length keeps you from getting caught in the lab equipment too.

WHAT YOU NEED

- Basic Robe on page 135
- newspaper
- pencil
- black acrylic paint
- copper, gold, and silver acrylic paints (optional)
- fabric-painting medium
- small, flat paintbrush, 1/4 inch (6 mm) wide
- alchemical symbols on this page and page 24
- iron

INSTRUCTIONS

1. Follow the directions to make the Basic Robe on page 135, but shorten the sleeve length. Instead of measuring from the wrist for the sleeves, choose a place halfway between the wrist and elbow as a starting point.

2. Lay the part of the robe you wish to decorate on a flat surface.

3. Place layers of newspaper underneath the places you'll be painting: in the sleeves, between the front and back, and along the bottom hem. This keeps paint from bleeding onto another part of the robe.

4. Use the pencil to lightly trace the alchemical symbols on the robe.

5. Mix a small amount of the acrylic paint with the fabric-painting medium following the manufacturer's instructions. Use the paintbrush to apply the paint mixture to the symbols. Write the name of the symbol below to help you remember which is which!

6. When you've finished decorating the robe, follow the instructions included with the painting medium for setting the paint with the iron (or hot dragon's breath).

Alchemist's Safety Gloves

These safety gloves work two ways. They protect your hands from harmful substances like bat bile or soap and water. They also prevent warts when you pick up a runaway toad in the lab. (Just kidding on that last part. I've heard that old tale since I was a young wizard, but it isn't true.)

WHAT YOU NEED

- newspaper
- any combination you like of fine-tip permanent markers, glitter or puff paints, large sequins, plastic jewels, and fabric braid
- hot-glue gun and glue sticks
- rubber gloves
- alchemical symbols on pages 15 and 24

INSTRUCTIONS

1. Cover your work area with the newspaper to protect it from spills, and set out the materials for decorating the gloves.

2. Give each party guest a pair of rubber gloves. If you wish, before the party you can lightly trace outlines of alchemical symbols.

3. Now the young wizards can decorate their gloves however they like! They can use the markers or paints to trace over the drawn-on alchemical symbols. They can add colorful, squiggly lines and shapes, and squeeze dots of paint along the fingers. With an adult's help, they can hot glue the sequins, jewels, or braid to the gloves for extra dazzle.

Alchemist's Spell-Catcher Safety Goggles

Wizards-in-training and student alchemists should always wear safety gear when they work in their labs. Who knows if that mixture of dried sloth toes, moon crystals, and salt water will explode? The wires on the goggles also help protect against harmful cosmic rays and spells cast by other wizards. Better safe than sorry! The goggles make great party favors, or guests can make their own at the party before they begin work in the lab.

WHAT YOU NEED

- impact goggles*
- brightly colored craft wire or pipe cleaners
- measuring tape
- wire cutters or scissors
- needle-nose pliers
- pencil
- large plastic craft beads in bright colors
- small styrofoam balls
- hot-glue gun and glue sticks (optional, but handy)
- dimensional puff paint, glitter paint, or acrylic paints
- small brushes (optional)

*You'll find inexpensive impact goggles at your local home improvement store. Goggles made of a flexible material, with ventilated sides and an adjustable elastic strap, are the easiest to decorate.

INSTRUCTIONS

1. Remove any hang tags and stickers from the goggles. Adjust the elastic strap if necessary for proper fit.

2. Measure and cut six to eight lengths of craft wire, each about 14 inches (35.6 cm) long. Set them aside.

3. Use the needle-nose pliers to bend a length of wire into a narrow U-shape. Thread the ends of the wire from the inside of the goggles through two adjacent ventilation holes. Twist the wire together a couple of times on the outside of the goggles to secure it.

4. Wind each end of each wire around the pencil to form a coil, or wind the wire in a flat spiral shape.

5. Add a bead to the ends of as many coils as desired. Use the needle-nose pliers to bend the ends of the wires to secure the beads.

6. Hot glue a few styrofoam balls to the ends of the wire coils as desired.

7. Use the dimensional puff paint or glitter paint to decorate the front of the goggles. Use squiggles, dots, or a continuous line to outline the lenses. Try not to put a lot of paint on the lenses, though a little won't hurt.

8. Set the goggles aside and let the paint dry while you play some games. Then let your wizard guests try on their goggles, adjusting the plastic straps if necessary. They can wear them home!

Wizard's Magic Flowers

A French alchemist named Vallemont (VAL-moh) once burned a flower. Then he mixed its ashes with secret chemicals in a glass beaker. When he heated the mixture, there was the flower in full bloom, floating in the beaker! He called it the Resuscitated (re-SUSS-ih-TATE-ed) Rose. You can try this amazing experiment yourself, using "secret" ingredients from the craft store and no fire whatsoever!

FIGURE 1

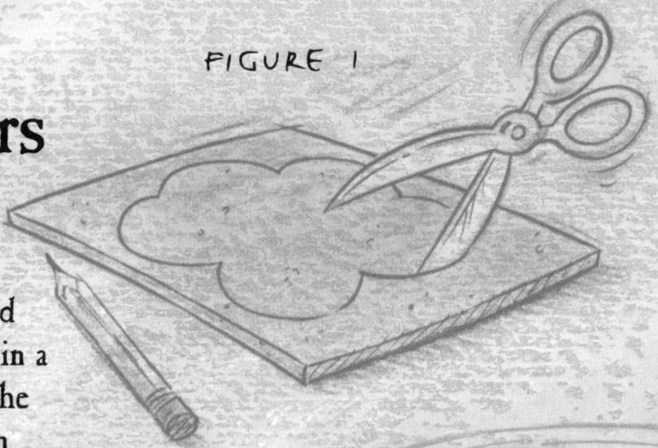

USE THIS FLOWER SHAPE AS A TEMPLATE.

WHAT YOU NEED

• flower template
• pencil
• white paper (optional)
• scissors
• compressed sponges*
• 1 large, clear glass container (or a smaller container for each guest)
• water
• magic wand (see page 138)

*Look for these near-paper-thin sponges in the stamping or painting sections of craft stores.

INSTRUCTIONS

1. Photocopy the template on this page, or use a pencil to trace it on a piece of paper. You may make the template larger or smaller so the flowers fit comfortably when they expand in the glass container. Make sure about this; a flower that's too large for the container spoils the effect.

2. Use the scissors to cut out the paper templates.

3. Place a template on a compressed sponge and trace around it with the pencil. Outline as many flowers as you need.

4. Cut out the flower shape. (figure 1).

5. Fill the glass container with water, and quickly wave your wand over the water while you chant the following spell:

Pansies are purple, iris are blue
Water makes flowers bloom
So do, I command you!

Alchemist's Gold with Handy Sorcerer's Pouch

FIGURE 2

My friend Agrippa was such a powerful magician, five kings asked him for help. But he was forgetful, and once paid his landlord with gold coins that became seashells! Your guests can make their own gold and carry pouch.

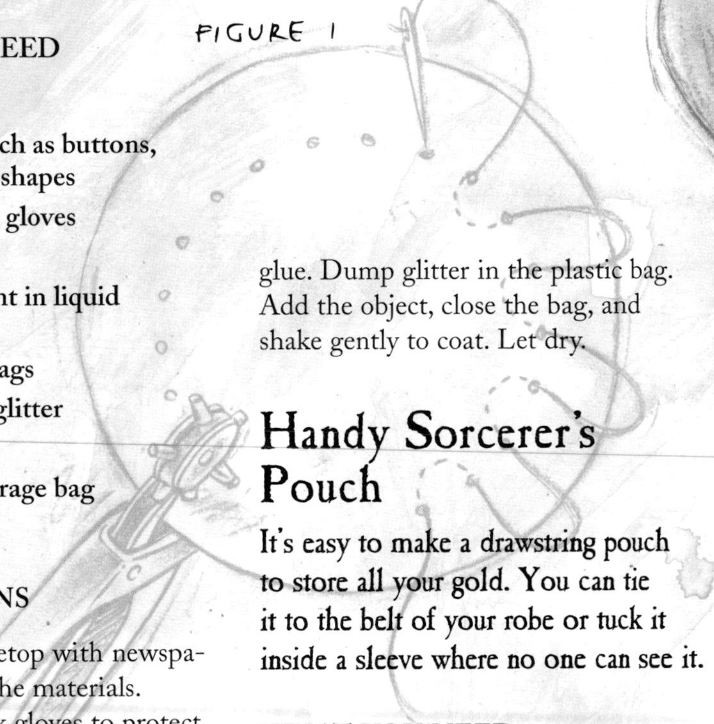

WHAT YOU NEED

FIGURE 1

- newspaper
- small objects such as buttons, pebbles, or pasta shapes
- disposable latex gloves
- paintbrushes
- gold acrylic paint in liquid or spray form
- paper grocery bags
- microfine gold glitter
- white craft glue
- plastic food-storage bag

INSTRUCTIONS

1. Cover the tabletop with newspaper and put out the materials. Wearing the latex gloves to protect their hands, guests can hand-paint objects or put the pieces inside a grocery bag and spray with the gold paint.

2. While the pieces are still wet, sprinkle them with a little gold glitter for extra sparkle. Let dry.

3. For extra-glittery gold, brush the pieces with a thin coat of the craft glue. Dump glitter in the plastic bag. Add the object, close the bag, and shake gently to coat. Let dry.

Handy Sorcerer's Pouch

It's easy to make a drawstring pouch to store all your gold. You can tie it to the belt of your robe or tuck it inside a sleeve where no one can see it.

WHAT YOU NEED

- 1 piece of cloth, felt, scrap leather, or chamois*, about 18 inches (45.7 cm) square
- circular template, such as a dinner plate or large plastic lid
- pencil
- scissors
- paper punch or large, sharp nail
- 1 yard (.9 m) twine, heavy string, or leather lacing

INSTRUCTIONS

1. Working on a tabletop, use the pencil to trace around the template onto the cloth. Use the scissors to cut out the circle.

2. Use the paper punch or nail to make evenly spaced holes around the edge of the circle (figure 1). Put the cloth's edge as far as it will go in your paper punch. Maintain this distance all around the circle.

3. Weave the cord in and out of the holes around the circle. Leave a tail of cord hanging from the starting point.

4. Match the ends of the cord and knot them together. Pull the cord to gather the material to close the pouch (figure 2).

*found in auto-supply stores

19

Fun Recipes for Young Alchemists

What's a good Alchemist's Party without things that bubble, ooze, smoke, and sparkle? Making potions, slimes, incense, and fireworks is a lot of fun for everyone, but young wizards should NEVER eat or drink any of the ingredients. Find an adult wizard (or nonwizard) to help with cooking things on the stove and to keep an eye on things in the lab!

Wurm Slime

Did you know that some of the earliest dragons were called *wurms*? They looked like very large snakes with dark skin that oozed slime. Young male wizards or anyone who likes ooey, gooey things will enjoy making this recipe.

WHAT YOU NEED

- metallic gel pen
- small plastic food storage bags with zip closing

- 17 ounces (510 mL) warm water
- clean quart jar with screw-on lid
- $1/8$ cup (28 g) borax laundry booster
- small mixing bowl or cup
- large kitchen spoon
- white craft glue
- green food coloring

INSTRUCTIONS

1. Use the metallic gel pen to label each plastic storage bag, "Genuine Wurm Slime." Set aside.

2. Put the warm water in the jar and add the borax laundry booster. Screw on the lid and shake until the borax dissolves. Allow to cool.

3. Measure 2 spoons of the white glue into the bowl. Add 3 spoons of water and stir.

4. Add 3 drops of the green food coloring and stir. Pour the mixture into the plastic food storage bag.

5. Measure a spoon of the cooled borax solution into each bag, one per guest. Each guest should zip the bag closed and knead with their hands to mix its contents. Everyone now has a bag of Wurm Slime to take home!

Dragon's Blood Potion

Dragon's blood has very strong magical powers, including the ability to change colors. Let each guest pour some into three empty glasses. Like magic, it becomes pink, green, and yellow! Prepare three glasses for each young alchemist.

WHAT YOU NEED

- adult wizard
- head of red cabbage
- knife
- stainless steel saucepan
- water
- strainer
- clear glass bottle with cap
- small clear plastic glasses (allow 3 per alchemist)
- metallic gel pen

- $\frac{1}{2}$-teaspoon (4 mL) measuring spoon
- white vinegar
- clear ammonia
- chlorine bleach
- blow-dryer

INSTRUCTIONS

1. With the help of an adult wizard, cut the cabbage into tiny pieces. Put it in the saucepan, cover with water, and heat to boiling. Strain the juice into the bottle. Seal the bottle and keep it refrigerated until you use it.

2. Use the gel pen to mark the glasses individually with a "1," "2," and "3." Make a set of three glasses for each guest.

3. Rinsing the measuring spoon between uses, measure $\frac{1}{2}$ teaspoon (4 mL) of the vinegar into glass one, $\frac{1}{2}$ teaspoon of the ammonia into glass two, and $\frac{1}{2}$ teaspoon of the bleach into glass three.

4. Use the blow-dryer to dry the liquids in the glass, leaving an invisible deposit.

5. Now let each guest take turns pouring the Dragon's Blood into a set of numbered glasses. As they pour into glass one, they should say, "*A dragon pink will never stink!*" With glass two, "*Dragons green are always mean!*" With glass three, "*A dragon yellow is a very fine fellow!*"

WATCH WHAT HAPPENS!

Presto, Change-O Potion

Command, "Presto, Change-O!" when you pour this potion from glass to glass. Watch it turn dark blue-black, then pour it into another glass, and it's clear again.

WHAT YOU NEED

- $2\frac{1}{2}$ cups (600 mL) water
- small saucepan
- 1 teaspoon (5 g) cornstarch
- mixing spoon
- large jar with a lid
- $\frac{1}{2}$ cup (120 mL) 3% hydrogen peroxide*
- eyedropper
- 1 tablespoon (15 mL) white vinegar
- iodine
- photographic fixer (also called hypo or sodium thiosulfate)**
- small clear plastic drinking glasses (allow 3 per alchemist)
- fine-tip permanent marker
- spoon or magic wand

*Available at drugstores.
**Available at photography stores.

INSTRUCTIONS

1. Put one cup of water in the saucepan. Add the cornstarch and heat on a stove, stirring with the spoon until the cornstarch dissolves. Add a second cup of water. Transfer the solution to the jar.

2. Use the permanent marker to number the glasses "1," "2," and "3."

3. Put the fresh cornstarch solution in glass number one. Add the $\frac{1}{2}$ cup (120 mL) of hydrogen peroxide and $\frac{1}{2}$ cup of water, and use the eyedropper to add a few drops of the vinegar.

4. With the eyedropper, put a few drops of the iodine on the bottom of glass number two. Wash the eyedropper thoroughly, then use it to put 2 drops of hypo on the bottom of glass number three.

5. Repeat steps 1 through 4 to prepare as many setups as you need for your guests, and arrange on the alchemy table.

6. When a guest is ready to perform magic, he should shout, "*Presto, Change-O!*"

and pour the contents of glass number one into glass number two (the one with iodine). The potion will turn a bluish black.

7. Shout "*Presto, Change-O!*" again, and pour the contents of glass number two into glass number three. Stir with the spoon or magic wand. The potion will become clear, then change back to bluish black in about 15 seconds.

Fairy Rose Water

Make this ahead of time for spend-the-night party guests. Each guest can sprinkle a little bit on a fresh herb or flower and sleep with it under her pillow. In the morning, if the flower looks fresh, that means she has a secret admirer!

WHAT YOU NEED

• 4 fresh roses
• 2 cups (480 mL) water
• saucepan
• strainer
• clean, empty bottle
• fresh wildflowers or herb sprigs (one per guest)

INSTRUCTIONS

1. Remove the petals from the roses and put them in the saucepan. Add the water and warm the petals over low heat until they become transparent. Let cool.

2. Strain the liquid to separate out the petals, and put the liquid in the bottle. Keep in the refrigerator until you're ready to use it.

3. Sprinkle the rose water on the flower. Sweet dreams!

Orange Peel Fireworks

Every wizard should be able to make sparks fly! But NEVER try working with a candle flame unless there's an adult wizard standing right there with you! Don't ignore this warning, or I'll turn you into a garden toad faster than you can say, "Dragon poop!"

WHAT YOU NEED

• adult wizard
• fireproof surface, such as an oven mat
• taper candle
• candleholder with sturdy base
• large rubber bands
• matches
• orange peels
• bowl or basket

INSTRUCTIONS

1. Cover the tabletop with the oven mat. Fix the candle in the candleholder and set it on the mat. Set the basket of orange peels nearby.

2. All wizards attempting this feat should now roll up the sleeves of

their robes. Slip one or two rubber bands over each arm to hold the rolled-up sleeves in place.

3. Dim the lights and light the candle. With the adult wizard supervising, each guest should take turns picking up a piece of orange peel and squeezing it, quickly flicking the oils from the peel through the candle flame. Leaping wizards, it's fireworks!

Nebuchadnezzar's Incense

Nebuchadnezzar (NEH-book-udd-NEZZ-er) was a desert king long ago. He commanded his court wizards to do something to cover up the smell of camel in the air. The wizards used spices from the royal kitchen to create this recipe.

WHAT YOU NEED

• 1 tablespoon (8 g) each of dried cinnamon, cloves, rosemary, sage, fennel, ginger, thyme, lavender, or dried ground orange peel (or a mixture)
• small heatproof dish
• benzoin*
• Fairy Rose Water on page 22 (optional)
• spoon
• 1/2 cup (224 g) aromatic wood shavings powder such as cedar, pine, or sandalwood*
• mortar and pestle, or a mixing bowl and large wooden spoon

- fireproof container, such as a flowerpot
- small quantity of sand
- round discs of charcoal
- matches
- adult wizard
- small plastic storage bags (optional)

*available at pharmacies
**available at herb shops, or use flaked cedar bedding sold at pet stores

INSTRUCTIONS

1. Put the spice in the mixing dish and add a few drops of the benzoin (and a tiny bit of rose water if desired). Mix well with the spoon, and let dry in the oven on low heat.

2. Combine 2 tablespoons (30 g) of the spice mixture with the wood shavings in the mortar or mixing bowl. Alchemists can take turns using the spoon to grind the mixture into a very fine powder.

3. Fill the fireproof container half-full with sand, and place a charcoal disc on top.

4. Spoon a little spice mixture on the charcoal. With an adult wizard's help, light it with a match, and enjoy the smell. You can also send guests home with bags of incense for their chambers.

Song of the Spoons

Do you know how your throat feels when you hum? Long ago, alchemists believed everything had its own voice or musical vibration. Even silverware! You MUST get an adult wizard to help with this experiment.

WHAT YOU NEED

- tablespoons, one per guest
- adult wizard
- 1 pair of oven mitts, the kind that cover the entire hand and wrist
- chunk of dry ice
- washpan or bucket

Instructions

1. Warm the spoons in a low-temperature oven, but not until they're red hot.

2. Dry ice can burn, so never, ever touch it! Have the adult wizard put the dry ice in the washpan.

3. Put on the oven mitts, and brace yourself! Press the warm spoon firmly against the dry ice. The spoon will scream loudly, then start to sing.

4. When the singing stops, select another warm spoon and start again.

Gaming

Gold-Oh! Alchemists' Game

Early alchemists tried to make gold from cheaper metals. Officially, they never succeeded. But I have to tell you that my good friend, the alchemist Nicholas Flamel (flah-MELL) became very rich indeed! Play this game like bingo, but use alchemical symbols instead of numbers. An adult wizard serves as game caller and awards "golden" prizes, such as pouches of Alchemist's Gold (see page 19).

WHAT YOU NEED (for the game cards)

- alchemical symbols on pages 15 and 24* (optional)
- photocopier (optional)
- paper
- poster board
- template on page 24 (optional)
- fine-tip permanent marker
- glue
- scissors
- wizard's hat (page 135) or basket

*Draw the symbols on the game cards yourself, or photocopy them.

WHAT YOU NEED
(for the game markers)

- large, dried beans*
- gold spray paint
- newspaper or empty cardboard box
- adult wizard
- small prizes

*You can also use checkers, shiny pennies, glass jewels, or wrapped hard candies instead of painted beans.

INSTRUCTIONS

1. Make several photocopies of the alchemical symbols on page 15 and this page. Set aside one copy of each symbol for the game caller.

2. Use the ruler and pencil to divide the poster board into as many 6-inch (15.2 cm) squares as you'll need for your party guests. Use the scissors to cut out the squares. Or, enlarge the template to the size you want and skip step 3.

3. Use the ruler and pencil to divide each square into nine equal squares. Make small pencil marks at 2-inch (5 cm) intervals on each side of the square. Connect the marks to create a grid. Trace over the grid lines with the marker.

4. Cut apart two or three photocopied sheets of the alchemical symbols. Randomly place nine different alchemical symbols on as many poster board squares as you will need and glue them in place. When each poster board square is filled with symbols, set it aside and let the glue dry. Cut apart two more sheets of symbols and put them in the wizard's hat for the caller to use.

5. To make the game markers, cover the work area with newspaper to protect it from overspray or use a cardboard box as a spray booth.

6. Place a layer of dried beans on the newspaper or in the cardboard box.

7. Spray the beans with paint and let dry. Turn the beans over and spray the other side with paint. Let dry.

TEMPLATE FOR THE GAME BOARD

HOW TO PLAY

1. Distribute cards and markers to the players. The adult wizard should explain the rules as described below.

2. When the adult draws a symbol from the hat, she should call out the name of the element and display the symbol to the players. If a player spots the matching symbol on his game card, he should put a marker on top.

3. Continue calling out symbols until a player covers a horizontal, vertical, or diagonal line on the game card. When that happens, the player should yell,

"I'VE GOT GOLD!"

(Calling out "Bingo!" doesn't count.) Award a prize and keep playing until the prizes are all gone.

AMALGAM   ANTIMONY   POTASH   ALUM

ADULT WIZARD SUPERVISION!

Bubbling Elixir of Life Layer Cake

Most people don't know how to make the real elixir (ee-LICKS-ur), a potion that gives long life. But some alchemists and wizards like me have lived many hundreds of years. Don't you wonder how we do it? Your guests will enjoy watching this cake fizz and froth before they eat it.

WHAT YOU NEED

Yield: 12 to 16 generous servings
• 6 fresh-baked cake rounds, each measuring 8 inches (20.3 cm) in diameter
• juice glass, 3 inches (7.6 cm) tall and $1^1/2$ inches (3.8 cm) in diameter
• chocolate cake frosting
• package of gelatin dessert mix
• lemon juice
• 1 tablespoon (15 g) baking soda
• colored candy sprinkles

INSTRUCTIONS

1. Cut a hole in the centers of two of the cakes. These holes should be the same diameter as the juice glass.

2. Stack the remaining cakes, spreading frosting between each layer. Top with the two cakes that have the holes in them.

3. Mix the gelatin according to the directions on the box. Let the gelatin cool for 15 minutes.

4. Fill the juice glass half full of gelatin. Add lemon juice until the mixture is $1/2$ inch (1.3 cm) from the rim of the glass.

5. Set the juice glass into the hole in the cake. If the rim of the glass sticks up over the edge of the cake, use frosting to disguise it.

6. Use the candy sprinkles to decorate the top of the cake in a pinwheel pattern.

7. Just before serving the cake, stir the baking soda into the glass. Foam will immediately start to pour out of the glass and down the sides of the cake. (The foam is edible, but it's not yummy like the cake!)

MAGIC Chameleon Eggs

The chameleon (ka-MEEL-yun) lizard can change the color of its skin to match what's around it, almost like magic. If you put an Interior Decorating Charm on the beast, it even adds a pretty pattern to the whites of its eggs. No time for a spell? Try this recipe.

WHAT YOU NEED

ADULT WIZARD SUPERVISION!

• white-shelled eggs, one for each guest
• red and yellow onion skins
• magic wand (optional)
• aluminum foil
• adult wizard
• large saucepan
• water

INSTRUCTIONS

1. Give each alchemist a raw egg. Wrap each egg in a single layer of onion skin, then wrap the egg with a piece of aluminum foil to keep the onion skin in place.

2. Wave the magic wand over each egg. With an adult wizard's help, place the eggs in the bottom of the pot, cover the eggs with cold water, and bring to a boil. Lower the heat to a simmer and cook for 10 minutes.

3. Drain the eggs and cool them under cold running water.

4. Guests can now unwrap and peel the eggs. See anything different?

NOW EAT!

Smoking Alchemist's Brew

ADULT WIZARD
SUPERVISION!

Every wizard's party needs an enchanted beverage. This recipe has extra power because you make it as a group project. I adapted the directions from the fabled, ancient cookbook *EDIBLE ALCHEMY*.

WHAT YOU NEED

- bottled lemonade or fruit drinks contributed by guests
- medium-size cauldron or soup pot
- long-handled wooden spoon or magic wand
- adult wizard
- insulated gloves
- flat disc of dry ice, large enough to fit under the cauldron
- newt eyes and toad marrow (or peeled grapes and chunks of peeled apple sprinkled with a little lemon juice to prevent browning)
- spores (powdered cinnamon)

INSTRUCTIONS

1. Ask your fellow alchemists to bring one drink each to the party (add a note when you mail the invitations). When everyone has gathered, pour each drink into the cauldron while reciting:

Magic cauldron, in you we pour
Fruits and fizz and spores and more
Help us make our charms galore!

2. Have an adult wizard put on the insulated gloves and place the cauldron over the disk of dry ice. Don't ever let the ice touch bare skin; it burns. Observe the magic vapors rising around the brew.

3. Add the newt eyes (grapes) and toad marrow (apple) to the cauldron, then sprinkle with the spores (cinnamon).

4. Use the wooden spoon or wand to stir the brew clockwise seven times, then serve.

ALCHEMISTS
I HAVE KNOWN

What would you do if you knew how to make all the gold you wanted? Long ago, alchemists tried to make gold by mixing cheap metals and smelly stuff like sulphur. They also hoped to find a potion to help them live forever. Legend says that some found the right recipe, while others blew themselves up with recipes that went wrong. I happen to know all this because we wizards make potions too. How do you think I've lived for 600 years, anyway?

The Egyptians were the first alchemists. Hmmm. Remember the gold treasure in the pyramids? By the Middle Ages, alchemists were every-where, working very hard and writing notes in secret codes. Many people swore they saw my alchemist friend Nicholas Flamel at the Paris Opera— 400 years after he'd died! (When I knew Nicholas, he was a real music-lover.) My other friend Paracelsus (PAIR-ah-SELL-suss) wasn't rich, but he was a great doctor and deep thinker. Quack doctors drove him out of town. But after he died, people kept seeing him!

Working from a very old book of Egyptian secrets, the Englishmen Edward Kelly and John Dee made sil-ver from lead and gold from tin. A greedy emperor put Kelly in jail, and he died in prison. But the Queen of England granted Dee a license in alchemy, and John lived a long, happy life after that.

The STORY of KING MIDAS

It takes a lot of hard work and study to become a wizard, you know, it doesn't just happen magically. People are always trying to cut corners, but things tend to go wrong when you haven't done your homework. This is the story of young King Midas and how he learned the hard way that you should finish whatever you start.

One day, Midas decided that he wanted to be an alchemist. Inspired by his eighth cousin (several times removed), King Solomon, Midas bought a book called *Alchemy for the Masses* and curled up in a chair in the royal library.

The first paragraph got his attention. It said that everything in the world was made of gold. Most things didn't look like gold, but only because they didn't know their True Inner Nature, said the book. The job of the alchemist was to help things realize their True Inner Nature.

Midas picked up a quill from the table. He held it up and said, "Your True Inner Nature is gold." Nothing happened. Midas took a deep breath and said, "Really, I'm not making this up. If you just accept the fact that you're made out of gold then you'll be gold!" Nothing happened. "Stupid book," Midas muttered and put it down. He got busy with

invading Syria and redecorating the dungeons. Midas told himself that he just didn't have the time to study alchemy. After all, a kingdom doesn't run itself. So the book went on a top shelf in the royal library, next to all the other books. (He'd read only their first paragraphs too.)

Midas didn't give alchemy another thought until many years later when he pulled a very wet Satyr (SAT-ear) out of the Pactolus (pack-TOE-luss) River. The Satyr was half-man, half goat and a good friend of the god Dionysus (DIE-oh-NIGH-suss). When the god learned that Midas had saved his friend's life, he offered to grant Midas one wish.

"I want to be the greatest alchemist in the World!" said Midas. "I wish that everything I touch turns to gold!"

"Are you sure?" asked Dionysus. "Wouldn't you rather have the recipe for the Philosopher's Stone?"

But Midas had never read Chapter Three of *Alchemy for the Masses*. He didn't know that the Philosopher's Stone would turn whatever it touched into gold. He thought the god was just trying to trick him. He stomped his foot and shouted, "No! I made my wish. Everything I touch turns to gold."

"All right," Dionysus sighed. He blinked his eyes, and it was done.

Midas picked a stone from the ground. It turned to gold! On his way back to the castle, he did it again. Gold, gold, gold! "Whew," Midas thought, "all this alchemy is making me hungry." So he set off to the castle kitchens, turning door handles and railings and walls to gold as he passed.

Midas found a sandwich in the castle kitchen. He picked it up, took a bite, and almost broke his teeth! The sandwich turned to gold as soon as he touched it. Midas saw a bowl of couscous (KOOS-koos) on the table. He took out a fork. It turned to gold. He picked up a big forkful of couscous and looked at it. It was still couscous. But when he put it in his mouth, it turned to gold! "Oh, no!" Midas wailed. "I'll starve to death!" Dionysus, who'd been watching, appeared. He took pity on Midas and told him to bathe in the river to get rid of his wish. Midas did, then he went back to the castle and ate and ate and ate.

King Midas never studied alchemy again, but from that day on, he always finished reading every book he started.

CHINESE Dragon Fete

Chinese wizards and dragons have been good friends—and guests at each others' parties—for thousands of years. The Chinese people love their beautiful, friendly, wise dragons. Hosting a Dragon Fete can be a little tricky, though. No fireball snorting or ear-shattering bellowing contests allowed!

Party Decorations

Make it clear that dragons live in your party room. Scatter around piles of Dragon Queen Scales (page 38), hang them from the ceiling, and glue some to your banquet tablecloth. You'll also want to hang up Chinese lanterns (page 31).

If you have your party inside, get an adult wizard to help you make dragon wallpaper from old bedsheets or rolls of paper. Add scorch marks by singeing the edges with a candle (do this ONLY with an adult's help, or I'll turn you into a fire newt!). Cut ragged slashes in the wallpaper, and dip a large comb in paint and drag it over the surface to make claw marks. Let dry and tack to the walls. Make a fireproof circle of bricks or stones in the middle of your banquet table. Put a small lamp, or an extension cord with a bulb socket and a red party bulb, inside the circle. Inside a clear bowl, place the eggs you've made for the Message from the Dragon Game (page 39). Balance the bowl on top of the fire circle so it's lit from below. Voila! A dragon's nest.

Arrange side tables so guests can play Dragon Wrestling after they've made their Dragon Hand Puppets (page 35). Two players sit at the table, don their dragons, and, keeping their elbows on the table, see which dragon can wrestle the other one to the tabletop. Since dragons often guard piles of loot, create a Dragon's Lair Treasure Chest. Follow the directions for Aladdin's Chest (page 64), but emboss it with patterns on page 32. Fill the chest with small wrapped prizes for game winners.

Your Treasure Chest needs its own Guardian Dragon. It's easy to make one out of empty boxes and paint, and it's a fun project for a group of kids too. Pick a spot on the floor next to a wall. Allow enough space so the dragon can lie behind the chest or curl around it. Don't be afraid to make it big. Use a tape measure to determine the length of your dragon, and make light pencil marks on the floor or wall. Lay a strip of plastic sheeting between the marks and at the join of the wall and floor, running it up the wall to protect it from paint. Tape in place.

Lay out cardboard boxes and tubes of different sizes to form the body, tail, and head, and hot glue them together (use an empty oatmeal container or shoebox to form the snout). Add claws, teeth, and ears cut from cardboard or carved from blocks of floral foam. Glue or tape in place. Cut a foam egg in half lengthwise. Tape or glue the eyes to the head, and paint.

Use tempera paint to paint your dragon's back green, its sides yellow, and its belly red, just like a Chinese mountain dragon. Dust with matching glitter and let dry. Use tubes of puff paint to sketch on scales, then dust with glitter. Don't forget to paint the ears, eyes, teeth, and claws (which look really good covered with black glitter). Turn the lights low, and see how real your mighty Guardian Dragon looks! Finally, set a fire extinguisher nearby with a sign reading, "Dragon Drencher."

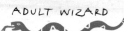
Chinese Lanterns

Festoon your party room with brightly colored Chinese lanterns. Make large ones and command them to float, or use decorative yarn to hang them from the ceiling. To decorate tabletops, place small container candles inside smaller lanterns lined with vellum.

WHAT YOU NEED

- piece of construction paper, 9 x 12 inches (22.9 cm x 30.5 cm) for a small lantern
- ruler
- pencil
- scissors or craft knife
- paper punch (optional)
- glue stick
- masking tape
- sheet of vellum, 8-1/2 x 11 inches (21.6 cm x 27.9 cm) for small lantern (optional)
- adult wizard
- votive candle or tea light and glass holder (optional)
- colored yarn (optional)

INSTRUCTIONS

1. Fold the construction paper in half lengthwise. Use your fingernail or the scissors handle to crease the fold.

2. Measure and mark points at 1/2-inch (1.3 cm) intervals along the two long edges.

3. Use the ruler and pencil to connect the points vertically.

4. Measure and mark a horizontal line 3/4 inch (1.9 cm) from the unfolded long edge.

5. Use the scissors or knife to cut the vertical lines up to the horizontal line.

6. Unfold the paper. Decorate the top and bottom rim of the lantern with Chinese calligraphy or designs (see page 32). You can also use the paper punch to add a pattern of holes.

7. Coat one of the vertical cuts with the glue stick. Bring the opposite cut over and press it into place on the glued side. If needed, use small pieces of the masking tape to hold the sides together until the glue dries.

8. If desired, roll the vellum into a cylinder that fits inside the lantern. Take the vellum out. Apply glue to the top long edge of the vellum, roll it into a cylinder and fit it in the lantern. Press the top edges together.

9. Ask an adult wizard to set the lanterns you've made over lit votive candles in glass containers. Don't leave burning candles unattended!

10. You can use larger sheets of construction paper to make bigger lanterns to hang from the ceiling (but not to hold candles). Punch two holes on opposite sides of the lantern top. Thread a length of yarn through the holes and tie the two ends together. Hang the lanterns from the ceiling or, if it's an outdoor party, from tree branches.

Chinese Wizard's Robe

A Chinese wizard was called a WU. He wore the beautiful silk robes of a scholar, a wise person who studied books. The robe featured pictures called IDEOGRAMS (ID-ee-oh-GRAMS) embroidered in real gold and silver threads. The robe of a wu who worked with plants and herbs might show a picture of a living tree. For a wu who studied the skies, a moon or sun. Many wizards chose a dragon for its all-purpose power, but they had to be careful because the Emperor didn't let just anyone wear dragons!

WHAT YOU NEED

- Basic Robe on page 135 made with richly colored, solid-color fabric
- newspaper
- gold or silver acrylic paint
- fabric painting medium
- paintbrush
- Chinese ideograms on this page
- iron (optional)
- 3 frog fasteners
- needle and thread

INSTRUCTIONS

1. Follow the Basic Robe directions.

2. At step 12 in the directions, cut a slit all the way from the neck to the bottom of the robe to create an open, flowing robe.

3. Place newspaper between the fabric layers before you apply paint to the robe.

4. Mix the paint and fabric medium in the ratio recommended on the package. Use the paintbrush to apply a broad band of gold or silver at the edge of each sleeve, the hem of the robe, and along the robe opening.

5. Choose any of the ideograms on this page and copy the motifs onto the robe as desired with silver or gold paint. Use a loose, brushy technique to imitate the style of Chinese writing called *calligraphy* (cull-IGG-gra-FEE). Let the paint dry, and follow the manufacturer's recommendations for setting the fabric paint.

6. Sew the frog fasteners to the robe, starting at the top near the neck opening.

月
MOON

龍
DRAGON

山
MOUNTAIN

雨
RAIN

日
SUN

木
TREE

Dragon Staff

All wise Chinese respected dragons and wouldn't dream of killing one unless it turned bad. In fact, Chinese wizards are rather fond of the beasts. They model their favorite dragons' heads in precious metals or rare wood and attach them to the tops of their staffs. Some of my wizard friends back in old China liked to play jokes on people by having their staffs suddenly roar and breathe fire just for fun!

WHAT YOU NEED

- Basic Staff on page 139
- head and ear templates on page 34
- tracing paper
- pencil
- scissors
- black fine-tip permanent marker
- 3 x 4 x 8-inch (7.6 x 10.2 x 20.3 cm) block of floral foam
- table knife
- small styrofoam balls, about 1 inch (2.5 cm) in diameter
- 8 x 8-inch (20.3 x 20.3 cm) square of cardboard
- toothpicks
- hot-glue gun and glue sticks
- newspaper or tissue paper
- plastic sheeting
- white craft glue
- small bowl
- plastic wrap
- gesso or acrylic primer
- acrylic paint in gold, silver, or other colors*
- paintbrushes

*Paint your dragon head to match your staff. Or, if you wish, paint it green or red just like a real dragon.

INSTRUCTIONS

1. Follow steps 1 through 5 of the Basic Staff instructions to prepare the rod portion of the staff.

2. Use the tracing paper and pencil to copy the side view template of the dragon head, and cut it out. Place the head template on the floral foam block and trace around it with the marker.

3. Position the foam block on the top of the staff and gently push the block about 1 inch (2.5 cm) onto the staff.

4. Remove the foam block. Set the block on your work surface with the traced shape facing up. Use the table knife with a sawing motion to cut away the foam around the shape you traced on the block. Use the knife to round the sharp edges of the head and to carefully narrow the snout.

5. Use a photocopier or tracing paper to copy the ear template. Cut it out. Create two ears by tracing around the template onto the cardboard. Cut out the ears, and hot-glue them to the sides of the head.

6. Gently push the styrofoam balls a

little way into each side of the head slightly below each ear. Then hot glue the styrofoam balls in the shallow depressions to create the eyes.

7. Cut out several small cardboard triangles. Press an edge of a triangle into the foam to make a shallow depression on the back of the dragon head. Then hot glue the triangle in the depression. Add as many triangles as you desire in the same way.

8. Tear the newspaper or tissue paper into 1/2-inch (1.3 cm) strips. If you want evenly torn strips, tear the paper by pulling up a strip against a ruler held down on the paper. Make two generous handfuls of strips and set aside.

9. Make a mixture of three parts of the white glue and one part water in a small bowl. Stir well.

10. After covering your working area with plastic sheeting or newspaper, dip one strip of paper at a time into the glue mixture. Run the paper between your thumb and forefinger to wring excess liquid from the strip. Apply strips to the head, overlapping their edges. Cover the head with one layer of strips, smoothing them as you work. Set the head aside to dry.

Cover the bowl with plastic wrap to prevent the glue mixture from drying out.

11. Put at least three layers of paper strips on the form. Allow each layer to dry overnight before adding the next layer.

12. Draw some teeth or fangs on the remaining scrap of cardboard. Hot glue the teeth to the dragon's mouth as desired. Cover the teeth with one layer of strips and set the head aside to dry.

13. When the final layer is dry, brush a coat of gesso or acrylic primer on the head. Let dry about an hour.

14. Paint the head gold or another color to match the staff. Let dry. You can also add other colors such as red for the tongue and eyes.

15. Use a generous amount of hot glue to attach the head to the top of the staff.

TEMPLATE FOR DRAGON'S HEAD AND EARS

Fighting Dragon Hand Puppet

Young wizards can put on a great battle with these puppets. I've noticed a few more things about dragons over the past 600 years. When they're not blazing fire or baring their talons, many look very mild-mannered. And most wouldn't hurt a fly, not on purpose. But when a dragon's fighting spirit comes out, watch out! This usually happens when one dragon tries to steal another's favorite nest, or if it steps on a mother dragon's eggs by mistake.

FIGURE 1

WHAT YOU NEED

- women's anklet sock
- ruler
- copy or notebook paper
- pencil
- scissors
- craft felt in red (for the mouth), a color to contrast with the sock (for the scales), and white (for the teeth)
- sheet of ultrahold, iron-on adhesive
- iron
- needle and thread in colors to match the felts*
- hot-glue gun and glue stick
- 9-ounce (270 mL) paper or plastic
- drinking cups
- wiggly eyes or yarn pompoms

*You don't have to sew this dragon, but I find that they fight longer battles if you hand-sew a line of running stitches around the edge of the mouth and down the center of the scales.

INSTRUCTIONS

1. Lay the sock flat with the heel side facing up. Fold the heel back toward the cuff, smoothing it so it lays flat (figure 1).

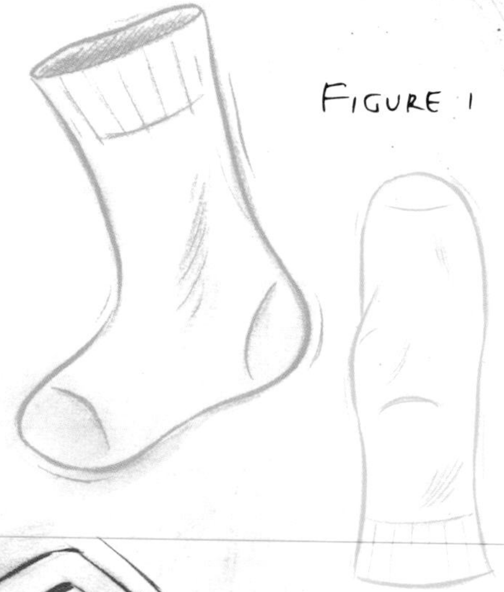

2. Measure the length from the heel to the toe. Measure the width of the sock. Sketch a rectangle the same length and width on a sheet of the paper. Round both ends of the rectangle, and use the scissors to cut out the rectangle.

3. Lay the rectangle on the red felt, use the pencil to trace around it, and cut out the mouth shape.

4. Lay the red felt mouth on the iron-on adhesive, and cut the adhesive to fit. Follow the manufacturer's instructions and use the iron to bond the adhesive to the mouth (figure 2).

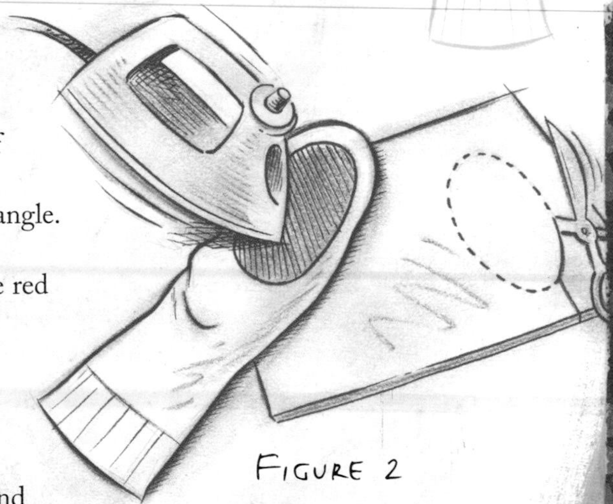

FIGURE 2

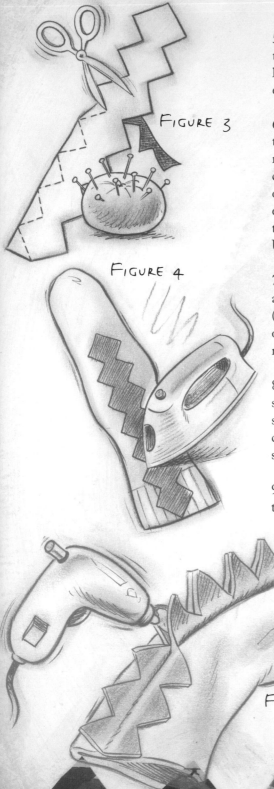

FIGURE 3

FIGURE 4

FIGURE 5

5. Bond the rectangle to the flattened sock. Allow it to cool while it lies flat. Hand-sew along the outside edge of the rectangle if desired.

6. To make the scales, cut out a rectangle of felt that measures approximately $2^1/2$ x 7 inches (6.4 x 17.8 cm). Fold the rectangle in half. Cut out triangles along the unfolded edges of the felt. Cut the triangles in toward—but not touching—the fold. Unfold the felt (figure 3).

7. Cut out a piece of the iron-on adhesive measuring $1/2$ x 7 inches (1.3 x 17.8 cm). Bond it to one side of the cut felt, centering it down the middle of the scales. Let it cool.

8. Turn the sock over. Bond the scales to the sock, starting with the scales near the end of the cuff. Let it cool. Stitch down the center of the scales if you wish (figure 4).

9. Hot glue the tips of the triangles together. Don't use too much hot glue. Hold the tips together with your fingers until the glue sets (figure 5).

10. Slip the sock on your hand. Put your thumb in the heel and your fingers in the toe end to form the dragon's mouth. Slip off the sock.

11. Use the scissors to cut the drinking cup in half lengthwise. Slip the cup half into the toe end of the sock. You've just made the snout (figure 6).

12. Try the puppet on again for size, and use the scissors to snip a slit in the cup if it's tight. Take off the sock and hot glue the wiggly eyes or pompoms in place close to the cup rim.

13. Cut out two nostril shapes from scraps of felt. Hot glue them to the end of the snout. You also can cut out tongue and teeth shapes and hot glue them to the mouth if you like.

14. Your dragon is now ready to go into battle. But remember, sometimes dragons lose things like teeth in a fight. Lucky for them that they grow right back!

FIGURE 6

Dragon Claw Power Jewelry

The curved claws and sharp fangs of dragons are rare, powerful, and greatly prized by wizards. In old China, one dragon claw necklace was worth more than its weight in the Empress's gold coins! It takes just one claw to guarantee that one magical wish will be granted when you need it most. Make your necklace with several claws, just in case you need the extra luck.

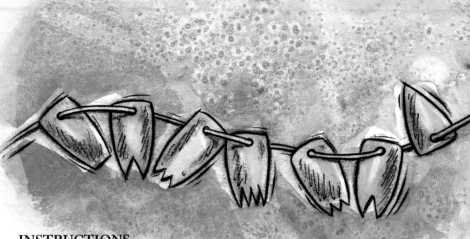

WHAT YOU NEED

- fake salon-style nail tips (the longer, the better!)
- nail file
- glitter nail polish in dragon-y colors (green, red, blue, or lavender)
- jewelry adhesive
- glue-on necklace bails or large jump rings*
- jewelry pliers (optional)
- sharp awl (optional)
- thin, satin cord (also called rat-tail cord), imitation leather cord, or inexpensive, base metal jewelry chains
- elastic bead cord (optional)
- French ear wires (optional)*
- nail polish remover, for cleaning up

*found at bead and craft stores

INSTRUCTIONS

1. Use the nail file to file each nail to a point, or file several points if desired.

2. Paint each nail with one coat of the nail polish. Let dry. Turn over the nail and paint the back side. Let dry. Paint on additional coats if desired, or add designs—stripes, dots, chevrons—in a second color if you wish.

3. Spread a small amount of the jewelry adhesive on the ends of a bail. Slightly spread the bail ends apart (the pliers help here), slip in the unfiled end of the dragon claw, and press the bail together. If you don't wish to glue bails to the claws, you can use the awl to poke a small hole in one end. Thread a large jump ring through the hole to hang the claw from.

4. Thread the claws on lengths of cord or chains.

5. For lots of dragon power, paint 100 claws. Let dry, then pierce each one with the awl. Thread them with the elastic bead cord and tie the ends together. You'll have a dandy power bracelet and enough good luck to share with your friends.

6. If your ears are pierced, paint two claws, pierce them, and thread them on French ear wires. As I understand young people say today, "You go, young dragon lady!"

Dragon Queen Scales

Did you know that as dragons grow, they shed their scales and grow bigger ones? If you're brave enough to enter a dragon's lair, you'll find piles of scales in different colors and sizes. But be on the lookout for huge, extra-sparkly ones. That means a Dragon Queen is nearby, and she may throw a hissy fit if you cross her! If you'd rather not battle a dragon today, you can make your own scales in different sizes, colors, and materials. Hang large ones from the ceiling or write secret messages on smaller ones and hide them around the house.

WHAT YOU NEED

- dragon scale template on this page
- scissors or craft knife
- pencil
- colored construction paper, cardboard, felt, oven liners, foam meat trays, or plastic bottles
- colored pencils, crayons, markers, acrylic paints and paintbrushes, or paint pens
- empty ball-point pen or stylus (optional)
- awl (optional)
- fishing line (optional)
- masking tape or thumbtacks (optional)

INSTRUCTIONS

1. Decide what materials you'd like to use to make the scales. Really large scales made from recycled cardboard boxes are impressive. Smaller, hand-size scales cut from yellow or pink foam meat trays are easy to toss around. You can also texture and emboss shiny silver scales made of oven liners.

2. Photocopy the dragon scale template on this page, making the photocopy larger or smaller as desired.

3. Use the scissors to cut out the template. Put the template on your chosen material, and use the pencil to trace around it. Cut out the scale. Repeat to make as many scales as you need.

4. Color and decorate paper or cardboard scales with anything you have handy, creasing construction paper scales down the middle to make them more three-dimensional. Use an empty ball-point pen to emboss scales made from foam meat trays or oven liners (see page 65). Scales cut from recycled plastic containers can be painted with acrylic paints or paint pens.

5. To hang scales from the ceiling, use the awl to punch a hole in one end of the scale. String the fishing line through the hole and tie a knot, then tape or tack the other end of the line to the ceiling.

DRAGON SCALE TEMPLATE

Gaming

Message from the Dragon Game

Wizards know that a drop of dragon blood gives us the power to understand animal talk. This game is based on riddles and on the little-known fact that dragons can also "speak" by leaving messages inside their eggs! Discard Secret Message eggs after the game—they're not good to eat.

WHAT YOU NEED

- $\frac{1}{2}$ ounce of alum*
- $\frac{1}{2}$ pint of white vinegar
- small bowl
- wooden spoon
- toothpick or fine-tipped artist's brush
- white-shelled, raw eggs
- saucepan
- hollow, plastic eggs
- small prizes or charms

*sold in pharmacies or in grocery stores with pickling supplies

ADULT WIZARD SUPERVISION!

?

INSTRUCTIONS

1. Add the alum to the vinegar in the small bowl and stir with the spoon until it dissolves completely.

2. Use this solution and a toothpick or brush to write an answer to a riddle on the shell of a raw egg (one per egg). Use widely spaced, block letters. Let dry completely, then boil the eggs in the saucepan for 15 minutes. Let cool.

3. Arrange the unpeeled eggs in a bowl. They'll look perfectly normal, but when the shell is removed, you will see the writing on the egg's surface.

4. Put a prize in each plastic egg, and hide them in different places around the party room. Make sure the place matches a riddle (see below). You can use the same riddle for more than one hiding place by placing prizes under two different chairs, for example.

5. To play, each player chooses a Secret Message egg and carefully peels it to read what's inside.

6. As an adult wizard reads a riddle aloud, the players should think about whether their secret message could be the answer to the riddle.

7. Any players whose messages answer the riddle should go look for the hidden prize eggs!

8. Keep playing until all the prizes have been found.

RIDDLES

"I lie around the entire day but I can never sleep. When you walk all over me, I never make a peep. What am I?" (rug)

"I can hold your favorite foods, including cakes and meats. But dish of peas or plates of sweets, I cannot ever eat. What am I?" (dining table)

"I have four legs but I can't run. Before you sit, do you weigh a ton? What am I?" (armchair or sofa)

"When day is done the sun goes down, and wizards go to bed. If you need light for magic rite, touch me and dark has fled. What am I?" (lamp)

"I have thousands of leaves but I'm not a tree. The words of many magic years rest inside of me. What am I?" (bookcase or bookshelf).

"My mouth is always open, but I have no teeth. I'm fond of many flowers, and anything in leaf. What am I?" (flower pot or vase)

"I play sweet tunes but have no harp, no fingers, and no flute. Your ears will hear my words most clear, unless you make me mute. What am I?" (radio or CD player)

Magical Imprisonment
of the Dragon's Egg

Sometimes you need to find a safe place to store a dragon egg before it hatches and runs amok in the laboratory. If you don't have a dragon egg, one from CHICKENUS DOMESTICUS (a plain old chicken) works just as well. Amaze your party guests with this trick, but make sure an adult wizard is around when you do it!

WHAT YOU NEED

- green food coloring
- water
- small bowl
- wine carafe*
- hard-boiled egg, shell removed
- spoon
- adult wizard
- scrap paper
- long fireplace matches

*Inexpensive wine carafes can be found at yard sales and thrift stores. If you can't find a carafe, use a bottle with a large neck.

INSTRUCTIONS

1. Mix a few drops of the food coloring with water in the bowl, and place the peeled egg inside. Let it sit for a few minutes or until it's green enough for you, then lift the egg out with the spoon.

2. Check that your egg just fits in the neck of the wine carafe. Take it out and set it aside.

3. Go find an adult wizard to help you. Scrunch up some scrap paper and push it down into the carafe.

4. Light the paper with a match.

5. Quickly set the egg in the neck of the bottle. *Abracadabra!* The egg will pop down into the bottle.

龍

Dragon Cookies

Dragons don't like to share their treasures, but they're polite party hosts and really good at making barbecue. My friend Leviathan used to bake these cookies with one blast of his fiery breath, but I prefer to use an oven myself. To honor our scaly friends, decorate your cookies with the Chinese ideogram for "dragon" shown above.

WHAT YOU NEED

- $3/4$ cup (170 g) vegetable shortening
- saucepan
- 1 cup (200 g) sugar
- $1/4$ cup (60 mL) light molasses
- 1 large egg
- mixer
- $2^{1}/2$ cups (350 g) flour
- 2 teaspoons (10 g) baking soda
- pinch of ground cloves
- pinch of grated nutmeg
- 2 pinches of ground ginger
- 1 teaspoon (5 g) ground cinnamon
- $1/2$ teaspoon (2.5 g) salt
- small bowl
- waxed paper
- cookie cutter
- 3 cookie sheets
- wire racks
- 2 cups (445 g) sifted confectioners' sugar
- 1 teaspoon (5 g) vanilla extract
- $2-1/2$ tablespoons (30 g) water
- small mixing bowl
- food coloring (optional)
- Chinese ideogram for dragon on this page
- decorating gel*

*found in the cake decorating section of the grocery store

INSTRUCTIONS

1. Melt the shortening in the saucepan over low heat. Add the sugar and molasses.

2. Beat the egg and add it to the mixture. Stir well.

3. In a small bowl, mix the flour, baking soda, and spices. Stir until well-blended. Add the molasses mixture and stir well. Chill for 1 or 2 hours.

4. Preheat the oven to 350°F (175°C). Roll out the dough on lightly floured waxed paper, adding flour to the dough and roller as needed. Roll the dough to $1/4$ inch (6 cm) thick.

5. Lightly grease the three cookie sheets. Cut out cookies. Place on the cookie sheets.

6. Bake the cookies 8 to 10 minutes. Make sure they don't burn!

7. Transfer the cookies to the wire racks and let cool.

8. Blend the confectioners's sugar, vanilla, and water in the cup to the consistency of icing. Color it with the food coloring if desired.

9. Spread the icing on the cookies. Let the icing harden slightly.

10. Use the decorating gel to copy the dragon ideogram onto each cookie.

Devilled Dragon Eggs

This recipe is a little tricky. First, use an Invisibility Spell to sneak into a dragon's lair. Next, steal some dragon eggs. Third—and this is the hardest part—escape with as few scorch marks as possible. Good luck!

WHAT YOU NEED

Yield: 24 servings
• 12 dragon (or chicken) eggs
• 2-quart (1.1 L) saucepan
• cold water
• kitchen knife
• small spoon
• ³/4 cup (250 g) mayonnaise
• 4 teaspoons (50 g) Dijon mustard
• 1 tablespoon (20 g) lemon juice
red or green food coloring
• 2 medium-size bowls
• whisk
• pastry bag with a 4-star tip,
¹/4 inch (6 mm) across
• pinch of cayenne pepper

INSTRUCTIONS

1. Put the eggs in the saucepan, cover with cold water, and bring to a boil. Turn down the heat to simmer for 10 minutes.

2. Drain the eggs and add cold water to cool them. Peel the eggs.

3. Slice the eggs in half lengthwise. Carefully scoop the yolks into a bowl and combine with the mayonnaise, mustard, and lemon juice.

4. Whisk the yolk mixture until it's smooth. Blend in a few drops of the food coloring. Put the colored mixture in the pastry bag.

5. Squeeze the yolk mixture into each cooked egg white, mounding slightly. Sprinkle the tops with the cayenne pepper and refrigerate.

6. Serve at room temperature, but never to a dragon.

Dragon's Breath Draught

When you drink this potion, please remember that it is not polite to set things on fire at a party.

WHAT YOU NEED

• cranberry juice
• 6-ounce transparent party cups or glasses, one per guest
• powdered dragon pearl (or baking soda)
• spoon

INSTRUCTIONS

1. Fill each glass halfway with cranberry juice.

2. Put a pinch of powdered dragon pearl into each glass. Stir briefly with the spoon.

3. The drink will start to bubble and foam. When the bubbles subside, fill the glass all the way up with more juice to make it drinkable for wizards and other nondragons.

Dragons in History

What do you think of when you think of a dragon? Probably green, scaly skin. Clawed feet and wings like a bat. An evil-looking little head on top of a long, curvy neck. Not to mention its ability to turn you into toast with its fiery breath if you get too close! That's one kind of dragon, but take my word for it, dragons can also act with kindness and courage. That's why dragon heartstrings make such powerful magic wands and potions.

Dragons are very different in different parts of the world. Asian dragons don't have wings or breathe fire. They look like they're made up of many different animals. They have a snake's body covered by fish scales in beautiful colors, the head of a camel, whiskers like a catfish, horns like a deer, and a mane! Asian dragons are kind and intelligent, and they protect rivers and bring good luck. When I met Chien-Tang (CHEE-in tang), the chief River Dragon in China, he had blood-red skin and measured 900 feet (270 m) long when he stretched out to take a nap. In old times, no one except the Chinese emperor was allowed to have a five-toed dragon pictured on his robes.

My Viking friends were always fond of telling the story of Siegfried (Sig-FREED) and the dragon Fafnir (FAFF-near). Siegfried was a handsome, courageous fighter, but I don't think he was very smart. An evil dwarf talked our hero into attacking Fafnir, a dragon with a hide so tough no sword or spear could cut through it. Fafnir guarded huge piles of gold and jewels that once belonged to the dwarf's father. The evil dwarf had another big secret, too. Fafnir was his brother, who had killed their father and then changed into a dragon to guard the treasure. Dwarves are the best blacksmiths in the world, and the dwarf reforged Siegfried's sword to make it stronger than ever. They hid outside the dragon's cave. When Fafnir came out for a bit of fresh air, Siegfried stuck him in his soft belly with the sword and killed him. After roasting the dragon heart in a fire, Siegfried burned his fingers on a bit of the meat. He licked his fingers, and suddenly he was able to understand the talk of birds in a nearby tree: The dwarf was planning to murder him! Siegfried struck first, killing the evil dwarf, and the treasure was all his. The magic powers of the dead dragon's heart had saved Siegfried.

There used to be different kinds of dragons in England. The Lambton Worm was a nasty one. A fisherman named John Lambton hooked it out of a river one day. When he got a look at the three-foot beast with a dragon's head and slimy black skin, he threw it in a well as fast as he could. Lambton left England to go on crusades with other knights, and many years passed. The worm grew so big it could wrap itself around a hill several times. It crawled into town to eat cows, chickens, and people. The villagers tried to kill it with knives, but it healed magically. Finally they fed the worm a huge trough of milk, and it crawled away to sleep. Lambton came home, saw what he'd done, and consulted a local witch for advice. She told him to wear spiked armor when he tried to kill the worm. If he succeeded, he must then kill the next thing he saw or his family would be cursed. Wearing his special armor, Lambton baited the worm to come after him, then slashed it into so many pieces it died. But when his father greeted him on his return, our hero of course couldn't kill him, and the Lambton family was plagued ~~~ bad luck for generations to come. Quite unfair, I thought!

When the Roman army invaded England, one of its best officers was very brave, and he rode a huge, beautiful white war horse. The people in a nearby village had been feeding their best sheep to a local dragon to keep it from attacking the village, and they were about to give it a young princess. (You never know, the dragon may have been angry that someone had stolen a bit of its treasure.) The Roman went to fight the serpent. He and his horse rode straight at it, and the Roman stuck it with his long, sharp lance, killing it. The English still remember the Roman and honor his memory. He's called Saint George and the red cross he wore over his armor is a well-known symbol of England. Saint George inspired many knights to go out to save princesses and slay dragons. Dragons are so rare now, they're almost impossible to find.

How to make a Handy Basilisk Protection Device

These make great party favors. The basilisk (BASS-uh-LISK) is a fearsome cousin of the dragon. It has a snake's body and a bright white spot on top of its head. Its poison is so deadly, it once crept up a horseman's spear after he plunged it in a serpent and killed the man! Even worse, if a basilisk looks you in the eye, you'll turn to stone.

For each guest, buy a palm-size mirror, a couple of ounces of polymer clay, acrylic paint and paintbrush, and glue at the craft store. Knead the clay with your hands until it is soft and warm. Pinch off bits of clay and roll it by hand into small snake shapes, coiled, straight, or wavy. Put the snakes on a cookie sheet and bake them in the oven about 15 minutes at the temperature listed on the package of clay. Let cool, then paint. Glue the snakes around the borders of the mirror to give it extra power. If you sense a basilisk is nearby, turn away quickly but hold up the mirror to the creature. It can't resist looking and will turn itself into stone instead of you!

The Story of Hoa, Liang, and the Dragon's Pearl

For hundreds of years, people in the West have feared dragons. They think dragons only use their fiery breath and huge size to battle knights and destroy villages. In the Far East, wizards and ordinary people know differently. Their dragons are kind-hearted protectors of precious, life-giving water, a substance we all need to live.

Every body of water, be it a river, lake, stream, or pond, has a guardian dragon. And every guardian dragon has a precious magic pearl. A wise dragon keeps it in its mouth, because if the pearl becomes separated from its dragon, all of a sudden things are Not Right.

This very thing happened in a village where a mother and daughter named Hoa (HWA) and Liang (Luh-ahng) lived. They grew rice, and that was all they had to eat. But one summer there was a drought, and the rice withered and died.

It seems that Shen Lung (SHIN LUNG), the river's guardian dragon, had been careless. He was a very old dragon who had lost most of his teeth. While flying about one day, his magic pearl slipped out from under his tongue and landed in the hills near the village. The pearl was separated from its dragon, and suddenly things were Not Right. You see, dragons make rain. With one fiery breath, a dragon knocks water from the clouds. Rain fills the rivers, lakes, streams, and ponds. Shen Lung lost his fiery breath along with his pearl, and the valley lost its rain.

Shen Lung changed form into a man and moved to the village beside the river he once guarded. To refill the stream, he had to find the pearl. And he had to discover a human as pure of heart as a dragon.

Hoa and Liang did not know about dragons and their pearls. They knew hunger. Hoa cried when she told her daughter to seek out relatives far away who could feed her. Brokenhearted, Liang began her journey. Walking through the hills, she came upon Shen Lung's magic pearl. She didn't recognize it, but she knew a beautiful pearl could be sold for a lot of money. She picked up the pearl and hurried home to her mother. The mother and daughter hugged and wept for joy. "We'll be rich!" Hoa exclaimed. "We'll be together!" Liang said.

Shen Lung had watched the family. Now he told them about dragon pearls. He showed his toothless mouth and spoke of losing his pearl. "I am too old to be a dragon again," he said, "But unless the river has a new dragon, the valley will become a desert and all the people who cannot leave will die of hunger and thirst." Shen Lung's words frightened Hoa. She feared losing the pearl and again being poor and having to send her only child away forever. "You do not need money as much as the valley needs rain," Shen Lung said.

At this moment, Liang knew what she had to do. She grabbed the pearl and put it into her mouth. Then, she screamed in pain. The pearl burned like fire in her mouth! Flames shot to her belly, then poured from her nostrils. The earth trembled. Liang grew huge. Her eyes turned red. Her skin turned into scales. Her head sprouted horns. Feeling an itch in her nose, Liang sneezed, sending a blaze into the heavens. The sky replied with a rain so heavy and steady the river was replenished.

Liang, the girl who became a dragon of the river, never left her mother's side. She always kept her magic pearl in her mouth, and all was Right again.

MERLIN'S BIRTHDAY PARLEY

Why not celebrate your birthday with a party at Camelot? My friend Merlin spent a lot of time at King Arthur's castle, and other wizards were always pestering him for invitations to visit. Arthur loved our practical jokes, but the queen got a bit frosty when we turned her lap dog, Lance, into a barking birthday cake.

King Arthur's Castle

Legend says that King Arthur lies sleeping in a cave, waiting for the time he will return to lead us to new glory. But you can make his castle rise right now and learn the names for the parts of a castle. Take it from me, this is important! Early in my wizard career, I visited the Archduke of Transylvania (TRANS-ill-VAIN-ee-yuh). Suddenly the guards yelled, "Troll invasion! Retreat to the donjon!" and I almost ran to the dungeon—er, basement.

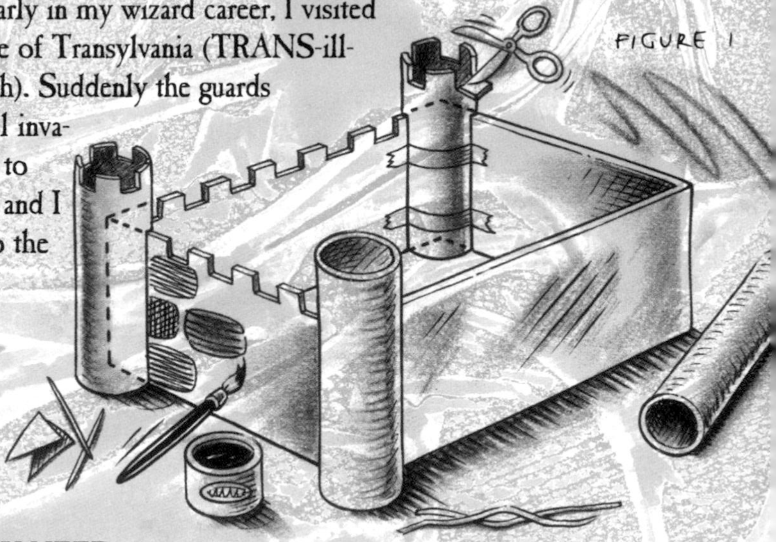

FIGURE 1

PARLEY DECORATIONS

When knights gathered for a parley, they met to talk and tell tall tales. Set your parley in the Middle Ages by decorating it like Arthur's feasting hall. Craft a castle for the table, and hang coats of arms from the ceiling. You'll want to make a Throne of the Realm (page 51) for the guest of honor—or whoever's fast enough to win the Throne in a game of musical chairs!

WHAT YOU NEED

- adult wizard
- large boxes
- 4 cardboard tubes, at least 2 inches (5 cm) longer than the boxes are wide*
- ruler
- pencil
- scissors
- box cutter or craft knife
- masking tape
- empty oatmeal box (optional)
- compass
- tempera paint in white, gray, brown, and black colors
- small paintbrushes
- small sea sponge
- awl or ice pick
- twist ties
- string
- scraps of construction paper in bright colors
- toothpicks
- mirror, big enough to set the castle on, leaving an exposed margin

*Gift wrap tubes work well. Use tubes at each corner of the castle and along the walls as desired.

INSTRUCTIONS

1. Ask an adult wizard to cut the top and bottom off the box. If you wish to make a double-sized castle, cut up the two boxes. Stand a box cutout on its side. Hold each tube against the box and use the pencil to mark the height of the box on the tube. Rotate the tube 180° and make a mark on the opposite side.

2. Use the scissors to cut straight up two sides of each tube. Cut up to, but not beyond, the pencil marks.

3. Slide a cut tube over each corner of the box and more along the middle if desired. (Leave space for the drawbridge between two tubes.) Tape the tubes to the box (figure 1). To link the boxes, stand them end-to-end and slide a tube over each join. Tape in place. Tape the oatmeal box inside the enclosure next to a wall to form a *donjon* if you wish.

FIGURE 2

4. Use the scissors to cut notches in the tops of the walls and the tubes to make *crenelations*. Get the adult wizard to use the box cutter or knife to cut long, skinny slots in the walls to make *arrow loops*.

5. Use the ruler, compass, and pencil to draw a door with an arched top in the middle of one wall. Cut it out to make the drawbridge.

6. Paint the castle and drawbridge white or gray. Let dry, then use the brush and sponge with black or brown paint to add rock outlines and texture.

7. Use the awl to make two holes in corners of the straight end of the drawbridge, and two matching holes in the wall. Wire them together with the twist ties (figure 2).

8. Make two holes on the arched end of the drawbridge and two matching holes in the wall. Lay the drawbridge down flat in front of the door. Cut two pieces of string long enough to connect the two holes, plus an extra 2 inches (5 cm). Thread the strings through the holes and tie large knots at the ends.

9. Cut matching triangles from the construction paper. Glue a toothpick between two triangles to make a pennant. Glue or tape it to the towers. Add cardboard "floors" if desired (figure 3).

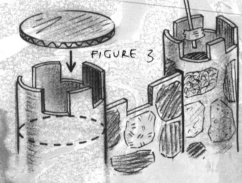

FIGURE 3

10. Place the castle on top of the mirror for an instant moat, and store game prizes inside the keep.

CASTLE Banter
KNOW YOUR CRENELATIONS FROM YOUR DONJON!

Arrow Loops .... Narrow slits in the wall for shooting arrows through

Bailey .... Courtyard inside the castle walls

Crenelations ..... The up-and-down notches in the upper edges of a castle wall

Donjon .... The inner stronghold of the castle

Drum Towers .... Round towers built into a wall

Dungeon .... The jail

49

Royal Coat of Arms

Your throne room or feasting hall should have its own coat of arms. And what is that, you may ask? Time for a history lesson! Many knights wore armor—good to protect against swords and spears, but bad if a knight on your side couldn't tell who you were. He might even take a swing at you! So knights started painting their battle shields to help identify themselves. This system is called HERALDRY (HAIR-all-DREE). Colors, and shapes called CHARGES, identify families. CADENCY (KAY-dense-EE) symbols stand for family members and their birth orders (page 137). These symbols are used on shield-shaped signs called COATS OF ARMS.

WHAT YOU NEED

- pencil
- shield templates
- cadency symbols on page 137
- scissors or craft knife
- poster board in blue, red, black, green, purple, gold, or silver, or cardboard and acrylic paints in the same colors
- paintbrush
- fine-tip permanent marker
- yarn or string
- 8 thumbtacks

INSTRUCTIONS

1. Use the pencil to copy a shield template onto the poster board or cardboard. Make it any size you wish. You could make shields 6 inches (15.2 cm) tall for table decorations or 2 feet (61 cm) long to hang on the wall.

2. Use the scissors or craft knife to cut out the shield. If you're using plain cardboard, paint it with the colors of your choice.

3. Choose a symbol to represent your family, and use the pencil to draw it on the shield. Use the permanent marker to go over the lines, and paint with additional colors as you like.

4. Are you the first, second, third, or ninth child in the family? Find your cadency symbol and add it to your shield.

5. Use the point of the scissors to punch a small hole in the top of the shield.

6. Thread a short length of the yarn or string through the hole, and tie a knot in the lower end. Use the thumbtack to hang the shield on the wall.

COATS OF ARMS

Throne of the Realm

Every king wanted a golden throne, but most used a finely carved wooden seat for daily use. Why not create a jeweled, silver throne for the parley's guest of honor? The throne will amaze and impress the other guests, and it makes a handy prop for several games (see page 57).

WHAT YOU NEED

- 2 large rolls of aluminum foil
- plastic deck or lawn chair
- cellophane tape
- hot-glue gun and glue sticks
- dinner spoon
- large plastic jewels, sequins, or flat glass marbles
- brightly colored cushion
- 4 tassels
- needle and thread

INSTRUCTIONS

1. Make as many 18- to 24-inch (45 to 61 cm) lengths of aluminum foil as you can from the roll of foil. Set aside.

2. Wrap a length of foil around one leg, pressing the foil to the leg contours. Press the foil against the surface with your fingers. If the foil slips, secure it with small strips of tape or with hot glue. Continue working up the leg, adding a new length of foil when it's needed. Tape or hot glue the foil in place if needed. Stop when you reach the bottom of the seat.

3. Cover the seat and seat edges with the foil, using longer lengths to wrap completely around the seat's top and bottom. Press the foil against the surface and secure with tape or glue, as needed.

4. Cover the back of the chair and the arms. If the chair back has slats, cover each slat individually.

5. When the chair is completely covered, use the back of the spoon to burnish the foil by rubbing it with repeated, short strokes. This will smooth the surface.

6. Hot glue the plastic jewels or sequins to the chair as desired. They look especially nice along the arms, back, and legs. (Avoid the seat, though. Even a king doesn't like sitting on prickly jewels!)

7. Use the needle and thread to sew the tassels to the four corners of the cushion, and place the cushion on the seat.

Treasure Grail

For many long years, the knights from King Arthur's court searched for the Holy Grail. The Grail was a secret treasure of great power. Legend says it was the cup used at the Last Supper, but no one knew what it really looked like. You can make your own multicolored, gold-flecked Grail by using paint and a clear plastic goblet.

WHAT YOU NEED

- newspaper
- heraldic symbols on pages 50 and 137
- sea sponge (or other type of sponge)
- acrylic paint in two bright colors
- paper plates
- clear plastic stemmed goblet*
- gold and silver paint pens

*You can adapt these instructions to decorate plastic dishes and cups for your banquet table. Paint the backside of a plate, not the side you put the food on.

INSTRUCTIONS

1. Photocopy the heraldic symbols of your choice and use them as a reference. Set them aside. Cover your work surface with newspaper.

2. Dampen the sponge with water and squeeze it out.

3. Pour about 1 tablespoon (12 g) of paint onto a paper plate. Dip the sponge in the paint, and then sponge color onto the outside of the goblet. Cover most, but not all, of the surface. (If you plan to drink from the goblet, leave at least 1/2 inch (1.25 cm) undecorated all the way around the lip.)

4. Repeat step 3 with a second color of paint. Cover all of the surface this time (except for the lip as noted in step 3). Let dry.

5. Use the gold or silver paint pens to draw the symbols on the outside of the goblet. Let dry.

6. Decorate the foot of the goblet. Use the paint pens to add stripes and squiggles from the foot up the stem and bowl of the goblet.

Merlin's Robe

Did you ever wonder where the old saying, "I've got a few tricks up my sleeve" came from? It was my friend Merlin who started it. He added pieces of cloth (sewn on three sides) to his robe. They made dandy places for storing things like salamander tails and thunderbolt starter dust. It's said that Merlin added a piece of cloth for each day of the year—365! And, when he found something that tickled his fancy, he added another. Merlin was always a practical fellow, and he called his invention a "poke it in the robe." When other wizards and nonwizards copied his idea, they shortened the name to . . . pocket!

WHAT YOU YEED

- Basic Robe on page 135*
- scraps of material (they don't have to match the robe)
- needle and thread, fabric glue, or fusible webbing
- iron (optional)
- fabric paints (optional)
- baking potato (optional)

*Modify the instructions as explained below.

INSTRUCTIONS

1. Follow the directions for measuring and laying out a basic robe. In step 12, cut the slit from the hem to the neckline.

2. Cut squares of different sizes out of the scrap material.

3. To make hidden pockets, attach the squares to the inside front of the robe or along the inside of the sleeves. Attach more squares to the outside of the robe. You may sew them on, use the fabric glue, or use the fusible webbing and a hot iron.

4. A beginning wizard might want to label each pocket with the contents, so he doesn't confuse his Elf Blasting Powder with Fairy Dust.

5. Use the fabric paints to decorate the robe. Stars and crescent moons are very Merlin-like, or copy any of the other patterns in this book, they're all wizardly! Follow the directions on pages 93 and 94 for making potato prints, or use the brush to paint them on.

6. Store all of your important wizard tools, potion books, CDs, and frogs in the pockets so you can use them when you need them. Just don't forget to put them back where you got them!

Morgan le Fay, Queen of the Fairies Robe

No one knows whether Morgan le Fay was King Arthur's half-sister or sister. Either way, she was a very powerful sorceress, and Merlin himself taught her. Her name means Morgan of the Fairies, because she was the queen of the Little People and may have been part fairy herself. Morgan was a gifted healer, skilled at using herbs. She helped save King Arthur's life after his last battle and got him safely to Avalon, also called the Isle of the Apples.

WHAT YOU NEED

- Basic Robe on page 135, made with fabric in a rich, solid color (candy apple red is a good choice)*
- apple and herb patterns on this page and page 79
- black and gold puff paint
- microfine glitter in gold and black
- extra-tacky adhesive (optional)
- plastic jewels (optional)
- Fillet on page 55 (optional)

*Modify the instructions as explained below.

INSTRUCTIONS

1. Follow steps 1 through 9 to measure and cut out the pieces of your robe but don't sew them together yet.

2. Choose the herb or apple patterns you'd like to put on the robe. Take them to a photocopy shop and have them enlarge the patterns and create iron-on transfers from the patterns.

3. Iron the transfers onto the robe pieces, or have the copy shop heat-set the transfers to them.

4. Continue following the directions for the Basic Robe to finish constructing it.

5. Place the robe flat on a table and smooth out any wrinkles. Use the black puff paint to trace over the outlines of the herbs, then immediately sprinkle with the black glitter. Let dry overnight, then shake off excess glitter. Turn over the robe and repeat on the other side if necessary.

6. Use the gold puff paint to trace over any apple outlines. Sprinkle with the gold glitter and let dry overnight. Repeat on the other side. Shake off excess glitter.

7. If desired, decorate the neckline and cuffs of your robe with the jewels. Lay the robe flat. On one side of the neck and cuffs, apply a blob of adhesive every 2 inches (5.1 cm) and press a jewel on top. Let dry. Outline the jewels with a "setting" of puff paint and glitter if you like. Let dry. Turn over the robe and repeat on the back side of the neckline and cuffs.

8. Make the fillet on page 55 if you'd like to have a crown. Add jewels to match the robe.

Fillet Crown

I remember back when a circlet (SIR-klett) or fillet (FILL-it) was a simple band of ribbon or a wreath of flowers worn on the head. Lovely Guinevere and the winners of Arthur's tournaments wore them. So did everyone when there was something to celebrate! Rich people wore fillets made of thin patterned metal, glittering with small gems. They were easier to wear than the heavy crowns of state.

WHAT YOU NEED

- oven liner or disposable cookie sheet
- ruler
- pencil
- scissors
- metal soup spoon
- heavy-gauge wire
- wire cutter
- needle-nose and flat pliers
- magazine
- clear cellophane tape
- rubber mallet
- hole punch
- two 18-inch (45.7 cm) lengths of thin ribbon
- dimensional puff paint, hot-glue gun and glue sticks, and jewels (optional)
- crescent moon template on page 137 (optional)

INSTRUCTIONS

1. Working with the oven liner, measure and mark a rectangle $1^3/4$ x 8 inches (4.4 x 20.3 cm). Cut it out.

2. Place the straight edge of the ruler about 1/4 inch (6 mm) away from the long edge. Then bend the metal against the ruler. Move the ruler and flatten the metal. Repeat on the other long edge.

3. Crease the bent edges with the back of the metal soup spoon.

4. Cut a 16-inch length (40.6 cm) of the heavy gauge wire. Use the pliers to bend the wire into a wavy pattern.

5. As shown on page 110, tape each end of the wire pattern to the magazine, then place the oven liner cutout over the pattern and tape it down.

6. Use the rubber mallet to pound on the metal. Go over the pattern several times.

7. Use the hole punch to make a hole at each end of the metal.

8. Fold one length of the ribbon in half, thread it through a hole, and bring its loose ends through the loop. Tighten the ribbon carefully. Thread the opposite hole in the same way.

9. If desired, decorate the fillet further by gluing on jewels or applying puff paint.

10. Use the ribbons to fasten the fillet around your head or your neck.

Magic Dagger

A wizard's magic dagger is a useful tool, but it's never used as a weapon against another being. Wizards use their daggers for things like chopping herbs for potions and cutting twigs to make new magic wands.

WHAT YOU NEED

- template on this page
- scissors or craft knife
- pencil
- cardboard (a recycled box works well)
- small paintbrush
- white craft glue
- heavy book
- gold, silver, bronze, or copper acrylic paints, or aluminum foil*
- blow-dryer (optional)
- acrylic paint, in dark brown
- paper towels
- plastic jewels (optional)
- hot-glue gun and glue sticks (optional)

*You can decorate the dagger with any of these materials.

INSTRUCTIONS

1. Photocopy and enlarge the template on this page as indicated or to a size that comfortably fits in your hand.

2. Use the scissors or craft knife to cut out the enlarged template, and use the pencil to trace around the edges onto the cardboard. Cut it out.

3. Trace around (only) the handle and handle guard portion of the template. Make a second tracing on the cardboard, so you have two. Cut them out.

4. Use the small paintbrush to spread a thin coat of the white craft glue on one side of the dagger handle. Lay one of the handle pieces on the dagger.

Turn the dagger over and glue the second piece to the handle. Lay the book on top of the glued handles and let them dry.

5. There are several ways to decorate your dagger. Paint one side with a metallic-colored acrylic paint, let it dry, then paint the other side. You can speed up the drying time by warming it with the blow-dryer. Another method is to lay the cardboard dagger on a length of aluminum foil and mold the foil around the dagger. A second layer of foil may be needed to cover it completely. To make the dagger look old, paint it with the dark acrylic paint, then use paper towels to wipe away most of the paint. Let dry, then hot glue plastic jewels to the dagger if desired.

ENLARGE 500 %

DAGGER TEMPLATE

Gaming

Birthday Parley Games

Use the Throne of the Realm (page 51) to play these three simple games. Merlin Commands is a wizardly version of the old standby, Simon Says. Merlin's All-Seeing Eye is a variation of I Spy. If you'd like a rowdier game, gather several chairs around your Throne of the Realm and play one of my favorites, musical chairs.

WHAT YOU NEED

(FOR MERLIN COMMANDS AND MERLIN'S ALL-SEEING EYE)

- Throne of the Realm on page 51
- An egg timer or small hourglass

Merlin Commands

HOW TO PLAY

1. The players should stand in a circle. The game leader decides who starts the game (choosing the guest of honor is a fine way to start). You can also choose the starter by adapting the old standby of "eeny, meeny, miney, moe": *"Eeny meeny miney moe, catch a wizard by his toe, if he hollers let him go, eeny meeny miney moe. Merlin commands Y-O-U."*

2. The first player, who is now Merlin, sits on the throne of the realm. Merlin then chooses the time keeper . The time keeper turns the timer and the game is on!

3. The words *"Merlin Commands"* must precede any command. The sillier the command, the better, such as *"Merlin commands, everyone stand on their left leg."* If Merlin says only, *"Raise your right arm,"* the players who do it have to sit down until a new Merlin is chosen. A new Merlin is chosen when the time keeper declares that time is up, or when only one player is left standing.

4. Start the game again. If one player was left standing, he or she becomes the next Merlin. If the sand timepiece ran out, choose the next Merlin as you did in step 1.

Merlin's All-Seeing Eye

HOW TO PLAY

1. Merlin is chosen and sits on the Throne of the Realm. This game can also be timed or played until players guess what is in Merlin's all-seeing eye.

2. Merlin must state, "Merlin's all-seeing eye sees something blue (purple, wet, small, you name it) in this chamber."

3. Players take turns, one at a time, guessing what Merlin has in his all-seeing eye.

4. The player who guesses correctly takes Merlin's place and the game starts over.

Musical Throne of the Realm

WHAT YOU NEED

- Throne of the Realm
- extra chairs (one for each player)
- music

HOW TO PLAY

1. Line up or circle the chairs, including the Throne of the Realm. Have each player stand behind a chair.

2. Take one chair away and start the music. Players must walk around the chairs until the music stops. When the music stops they can sit in any of the chairs except the Throne of the Realm. If a player sits on the Throne by mistake, he or she is declared "out." When you start the next round, remove another chair.

3. Continue playing (and removing chairs) until you have two players, one chair, and the Throne. The winner is the player who sits in the one remaining chair. The winner then gets to sit on the Throne.

Search for the Grail Treasure Hunt

Since King Arthur's knights spent so much time looking for the Grail, why not have a game in which guests look for the Grail and other prizes too?

WHAT YOU NEED

- Treasure Grail (page 52)
- small prizes,
- adult wizard

HOW TO PLAY

1. First make the Treasure Grail.

2. Hide the Grail and the other prizes in the hiding places listed in the Message from the Dragon Game on page 39.

3. The adult wizard should now read each riddle, one by one, from the Message from the Dragon Game. Keep playing until everyone has guessed at least one answer and found a prize. The person who finds the Grail gets to keep it!

Feasting

ADULT WIZARD
SUPERVISION!

Ladon's Apple Cake

Ladon was a Greek dragon who guarded the Tree of Golden Apples. He claims this recipe tastes best if you use real gold apples, but that's one cake I wouldn't sink my teeth into.

WHAT YOU NEED

Yield: 8 servings

- 10-inch (25.4 cm) glass pie pan
- 3 medium-size, tart apples
- 1 teaspoon (5 mL) lemon juice
- 3/4 cup (150 g) plus 3 tablespoons (15 mL) granulated sugar
- 2 teaspoons (30 mL) cinnamon
- 3/4 cup (250 g) unsalted butter, cut in pieces
- small saucepan
- medium bowl
- 2 large eggs
- 1 cup (150 g) flour
- wire rack
- vanilla ice cream

INSTRUCTIONS

1. Preheat the oven to 350°F (180°C). Butter the pie pan and set it aside.
2. Peel, core, and slice the apples into thin pieces. Toss them with the lemon juice, two tablespoons of sugar, and the cinnamon. Spread them in the bottom of the pie pan.

3. Melt the butter in a small saucepan over medium heat. Cook it for about 7 minutes, until lightly golden. Pour the butter into a bowl.

4. Stir in the sugar. Beat in the eggs and add the flour. Mix until smooth.

5. Spoon the batter into the pie pan on top of the apples. Spread the batter evenly and sprinkle the top with the last tablespoon of sugar.
6. Bake for 40 to 45 minutes, until the cake is light golden and crusty.

7. Cool the cake in the pan on a wire rack. Serve with the ice cream.

Pegasus's Caramel Apples

It takes more than your usual apple to satisfy Pegasus (PEG-ah-SUSS). He's the white, winged horse who lives in the clouds. He loves caramel so much, he'll swoop down in a flash to sneak a snack.

WHAT YOU NEED

Yield: 8 servings
• adult wizard
• 8 medium apples
• 8 wood sticks
• butter
• cookie sheet
• 1 cup (110 g) coarsely chopped nuts
• small bowl
• 21 ounces (about 75 pieces) caramel
• 3 tablespoons (45 mL) water
• heavy saucepan
• spoon

INSTRUCTIONS

1. Wash and dry the apples. Remove the stems and insert a wood stick into each of the apples.

2. Butter the cookie sheet and set the apples on it.

3. Chop the nuts. (Instead of trying out your new Super-Slicer Spell, please get an adult to do this). Put them in a small bowl and set aside.

4. Put the caramels and the water in the saucepan. Heat them over medium-low heat, stirring frequently, until the caramels are melted.

5. Dip each apple into the hot caramel. Use the spoon if neccessary to apply the caramel to the top of the apple. Let the excess caramel drip off.

6. Set the apple very briefly into the bowl of nuts, then place it on the cookie sheet.

7. Let stand for 30 minutes or until firm.

Sword in the Stone Icy Treats

With this frozen treat, everybody gets to be a young Arthur. This treat is best served to older party guests who know that they should never fly or run while eating.

WHAT YOU NEED

Yield: 12 servings
• 12 small plastic cocktail swords
• 12 maraschino cherries
• ice cube tray
• water or fruit juice

INSTRUCTIONS

1. Stick a cocktail sword into each cherry so the sword is held firmly in place.

2. Put each cherry in a compartment of the ice cube tray, and add the water or juice.

3. Freeze for at least two hours, then remove and serve. (No sword swallowing, please.)

Lady of the Lake Spicy Cider

Did you know Merlin was imprisoned in a tree for 12 centuries? When he finally escaped, the Lady of the Lake found him. (She's the same person who gave King Arthur the sword Excalibur.) She nursed Merlin back to health with this cider. It's delicious, but most things are when you haven't eaten in 1,200 years.

WHAT YOU NEED

Yield: 8 servings
• 2 quarts (2.2 L) apple cider
• ½ cup (100 g) confectioner's sugar
• 2 pinches of nutmeg
• 2 pinches of cinnamon
• 1 pinch of powdered ginger
• large pot
• wooden spoon

INSTRUCTIONS

1. Combine the apple cider, confectioner's sugar, nutmeg, cinnamon, and ginger in the pot. Stir with the wooden spoon.

2. Simmer the cider for about 15 minutes over low heat. Be careful not to boil it.

3. Serve the cider warm.

StoryTelling Time

THE STORY OF KING ARTHUR and the Sword in the Stone,

AS TOLD BY MERLIN HIMSELF

Everyone knows that I'm a wizard, but they're wrong to say I used a magic spell to make the famous Sword in the Stone. Here's the story of what really happened.

On the night Arthur was born to his parents, the King and Queen of England, I took him into hiding. I hid Arthur at the castle of Sir Ector, to be brought up with Ector's son, Kay. Sadly, Arthur's father was killed in a battle, and England was without a king for 13 long years. But at least I'd made sure the boy Arthur was hidden and safe from his enemies.

But I can't take credit for the sword. It just appeared on Christmas Day, stuck in a huge rock in the churchyard of the Archbishop of London. On the side, written in gold letters, were the words, "Whoever shall pull this sword from this stone is the True King of England." (If I'd made the sword, I would have written something much more clever on the rock, and it would have rhymed, too.) Anyway, the Archbishop sent messengers everywhere to announce a tournament and a contest. And the contest had the greatest prize of all! Any knight who could pull the sword out of the stone would become king.

I made sure a messenger went by swift horse to Sir Ector, even though I had to turn myself into the horse to do it! Ector and Kay clapped on their armor and sped to London, bringing Arthur along as their squire. Kay entered the first fight of the tournament—a battle with a very large knight. The fight had barely begun when Kay's sword made a nasty creaking sound and broke in half! (Oh, did I do that? Oops.) Arthur ran off to find a new sword for Kay.

As Arthur ran by the church, a glint of sunlight shone from the sword in the stone, catching his eye. The churchyard was empty. Who would notice, Arthur thought, if he borrowed the sword? He'd return it as soon as Kay was done. He reached out, wrapped both hands around the handle, and pulled. The sword slid out of the rock, and Arthur hurried back to the tournament and gave it to Kay. Kay recognized the sword, turned around and presented it to the Archbishop, and claimed the throne for himself!

I'd turned myself into a falcon so I could fly around and keep an eye on things. When I heard Kay tell his big fib, I called out, but people heard only my harsh bird's cry! Fortunately, the Archbishop wisely insisted that Kay do it again. The sword was put back in the rock and Kay pulled and pushed and shouted at it, but it would not budge. The Archbishop asked who had really taken the sword out of the stone. Arthur stepped forward, put his hands on the handle, closed his eyes, and—you guessed it—pulled it right out, its blade bright as flame! I changed back into my usual Merlin shape and revealed the secret of who Arthur's parents really were. Arthur was crowned that very day, and he ruled Britain as a good and wise king for the rest of his life, with a bit of help from me. But that's another story.

MERLIN, My Magical Friend
AS TOLD BY THE WIZARD

I knew Merlin quite well, and it's true that he was the most powerful wizard of us all. He went to the Other Side a long time ago, but sometimes I swear I hear him chuckling when I walk by a grove of oak trees or when an owl flies by my window. It would be just like him to come back secretly to keep an eye on things. Wizards never quite give up wanting to make things right in the world, you know. Plus, they rarely miss a chance to gather for a song and a drink of cider, and Merlin was no different.

Merlin was a Druid, one of the famous wise men of the old Celtic tribes. His mother was a Welsh princess and his father was, well, supernatural. Merlin could see the future, appear and disappear in the wink of an eye, cast spells, and make magic. He decided very early on that he would use his powers only for good, never evil.

Merlin gave advice to several British kings, who did well to listen to him. Legend says Merlin used his powers to bring giant stones across the sea from Ireland. They still stand today in a place in England called Stonehenge. Merlin also used magic to bring together Arthur's parents so that Arthur would be born. Merlin was teacher to young Arthur, and some people say he arranged for Arthur to pull the famous sword from the stone. Merlin also talked the Lady of the Lake into giving Arthur her magical sword, Excalibur. Merlin came up with the idea of the Round Table, and he helped Arthur to govern Camelot and defend his kingdom against invaders. Then one day, he was gone.

Many stories try to explain what happened to Merlin. Some say Merlin went with Arthur to the magical Isle of Avalon. Others say that he's trapped in a hawthorn tree, put there by the sorceress Nimue. But in my humble opinion, a wizard as powerful as Merlin wouldn't stay stuck forever. I like to believe the story that says he waits in a crystal cave, guarding the True Throne of the Realm, where Arthur will sit again one day.

Open, Sesame!
ALADDIN'S CAVE PARTY

Here's how to give a desert wizards' party inspired by Aladdin. He's the lucky lad who rubbed a bottle, found a genie, and the rest was history. We wizards know that deserts are simply jam-packed with genies. They're always popping out of sand dunes and twisting camels' tails!

Aladdin's Treasure Chest

Every Aladdin's Cave needs treasure, and this chest is great for holding gift-wrapped prizes for your party guests. After the party, use the chest to store your wizard's robes, dragon eggs, and other magical items you want to keep secret from nonwizard eyes.

Let's pretend you're inside the home of Bedouins (BED-oo-ins), the Arab desert tribes. They live in huge tents that they put up and take down whenever they want. To turn your party room into a "tent," start with a pile of sheets or use 8 foot (2.4 m) lengths of wide fabric. Use a needle and thread to run a large basting stitch across one end of each piece of fabric or sheet. Pull the thread to gather the fabric and tie a knot in it. Tack the fabrics to the wall with the gathered ends at the top, overlapping the side edges. Pile pillows and scatter rugs on the floor for seating. Put a few large baskets with lids in the corners of the room. Add signs stating, "Basket Contains Charmed Invisi-Bull Snakes, Open at Your Own Risk!"

Decorate your banquet table with Magic Carpets that guests can take home. (If a wizard needs to fly someplace fast, this solo-size carpet will work just fine. It's the power of the wizard's Flying Charm that does the work, not the size of the carpet.) If you like, add Genie Bottles (page 67) to the table.

The most important thing in the party room will be the Desert Wizard's Lair. Remember when you built forts out of furniture and blankets? That's exactly what you'll do here. Turn chairs or small tables on their sides and move them together, leaving a space big enough to hold a Treasure Chest and one crouching party guest. Cover the inside and outside of the structure with rugs, sheets, or fabrics in solid colors or stripes. Put rugs on the floor and place the chest inside. If you have a camel, park one outside the tent, but be sure to open the window. (There's a reason wizards use Camel's Breath Bombs to keep away nasty genies.)

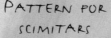

PATTERN FOR SCIMITARS

WHAT YOU NEED

- corrugated cardboard storage box with removable lid*
- acrylic paint
- paintbrushes
- heavy aluminum foil oven liner
- scissors
- ball-point pen
- ruler
- white craft glue
- chopstick
- scrap paper

*available at discount and hardware stores

INSTRUCTIONS

1. Assemble the storage box. Choose a color and paint the outside of the box. Let it dry.

2. Draw eight rectangles measuring 2 x 6 inches (5 x 15 cm) on an aluminum foil oven liner. Cut them out.

Round the
corners of each
rectangle. Use the ball-
point pen to draw several small circles
at the ends of each rectangle; these become the "nail heads." Press hard with
the pen when you outline the nail heads, then turn over the foil and rub hard
(emboss) inside each circle. This makes them stand out. Fill the circles with
the white craft glue and let them dry overnight. This will keep your nail
heads from being easily dented.

3. Glue two rectangles around each corner of the trunk.

4. Cut extra shapes of your choice from the oven liner, and emboss them
with Arabic patterns. Photocopy the scimitar, minaret or hamsa patterns in
the sizes desired. Place the photocopy on top of the oven liner. Use the
ball-point pen to trace over the pattern, pressing down firmly. Remove the
photocopy, and turn over the oven liner. Emboss the pattern with the pen or
a chopstick. Fill the embossed pattern with white craft glue and let it dry.

5. Cut out your embossed patterns and glue them to the box. Fill the box
with prizes or party favors.

6. After the party, if you'd like to add your name or a secret word to the
trunk, copy it on a piece of scrap paper. Then hold the paper against a window, with the writing side pressed against the glass. Trace the reversed letters
with the pencil. Use this pattern to emboss another piece of oven liner, then
glue it on the trunk lid.

Magic Carpets

When desert nomads set up camp,
they unroll their carpets and use
them to cover floors and make tent
"walls." The rugs have different patterns, including flowers, vines, and
the towers called minarets (MEN-
ah-RETZ). The hamsa, or Hand of
Fatima (FA-tuh-muh), is very popular because it protects against the
evil eye. Arabian wizards sprinkled
their carpets with special dust to
make them fly. Alas, the vacuum
cleaner put an end to many magic
carpets. All because some people
think rugs should be cleaned!

WHAT YOU NEED

• sheets of colored construction
paper, 12 x 18 inches (30.5 x 45.7 cm)

• precut felt, 9 x 12 inches
(22.9 x 30.5 cm) (optional)

• scissors

• decorative-edge scissors (optional)

• minaret and hamsa on pages 66
and 137

• pencil

• white craft glue or fusible webbing

• iron (optional)

continued

INSTRUCTIONS

1. Create a fringe for your magic carpet by using the scissors to cut the fringe about 1 inch (2.5 cm) deep along each end of the paper or felt. Use the decorative-edge scissors to make a pattern on the fringe if desired.

2. Use a photocopier to make several copies of each pattern template.

3. Cut out the patterns. Place the patterns on different colors of construction paper or felt. Use the pencil to trace around the patterns. Cut out the patterns.

4. Lay the cut-out shapes in a pleasing arrangement on the paper or felt. Rug designs were always symmetrical, but your design doesn't have to be.

5. When you're satisfied with your layout, use the white craft glue to adhere the shapes to the carpet, or attach them using the fusible webbing and iron.

HAMSA

Desert Wizard Robe and Headdress

My desert wizard friends liked simple clothing and didn't wear fancy dress. A typical wizard wore a striped robe called a JELLABA (GEL-ah-bah), and a headdress known as a KAFFIYEH (KAH-fuh-YAY). The headdress was held in place with an band of cord. You can decorate yours with colorful threads or beads (blue beads ward off the evil eye). The robe will keep you warm during cold desert nights. The headdress protects against the hot desert sun or sandstorms stirred up by an angry genie.

Making the Jellaba

WHAT YOU NEED

• Basic Robe on page 135, but substitute brightly striped fabric (or plain cotton fabric decorated with fabric paints)

INSTRUCTIONS

1. Follow the directions for making the Basic Robe up to step 12. Lay the robe out so that the stripes run up and down, not crosswise. If you use a plain fabric, use fabric paint to paint stripes on it.

2. At step 12 in the Basic Robe directions, extend the slit from the neckline down to the hem to create an open, flowing robe.

Making the Kaffiyeh

WHAT YOU NEED

• 2 lengths of thick cord or yarn, each measuring 36 inches (91 cm)
• wooden craft beads with holes large enough to thread the cord or yarn through
• piece of cloth, 36 x 36 inches (91 x 91 cm), striped, patterned or plain

INSTRUCTIONS

1. Tie the two cords at one end with an overhand knot.

2. Tie an overhand knot about 12 inches (15 cm) from the first, thread a bead onto the cord, then tie another knot to secure the bead.

3. Thread additional beads as desired on the cord and secure each one with a simple overhand knot.

4. Leave about 12 inches (15 cm) of the cord unbeaded at the end. Tie an overhand knot at the end.

5. Fold the square of cloth in half to form a triangle.

6. Place the folded triangle on your head, with a point on each shoulder and one down the back.

7. Adjust the cloth so that the folded edge comes about halfway down your forehead. Wrap the cords around your head with the beads in front. Tie the loose ends at the back.

Genie Bottle

This bottle is handy to have in case you find a genie floating around. Take the genie by surprise and command it to get into the bottle. (It's easier if you're wearing a Genie Command Ring, see page 68.) If your genie is out running an errand for you, you can use the bottle to carry water when you cross a desert.

WHAT YOU NEED

• nicely shaped, plastic bottle (dish-washing liquid bottles work well)*
• patterns on pages 66 and 137
• scissors
• fine-tip permanent marker
• acrylic paints in rich colors
• small artist's paintbrush
• puff paint
• sequins or plastic jewels
• hot-glue gun and glue sticks
• cork or stopper (optional)

*You can also use a glass bottle. To decorate it, use glass paints and follow the manufacturer's recommendations for curing the paint.

continued
INSTRUCTIONS

1. Wash and rinse your bottle so it's extra clean. Dry it thoroughly inside and out.

2. Use the patterns as guides. Photocopy and cut out the patterns, then use the marker to trace them on the bottle or copy them freehand.

3. Use the acrylic paint to decorate the bottles, and use the puff paint to trace around the patterns or to make extra designs. Let dry.

4. Hot glue a row of sequins or plastic jewels on the bottle, or cover the entire surface.

5. Just to be on the safe side, use puff paint to add your name to the design. If some thief of Baghdad steals your bottle, you'll be able to identify it right away!

6. If you wish, replace the bottle cap with a cork or stopper that fits the neck of the bottle. Insert the cork, and mark the point where it extends from the bottle neck. Use paint or jewels to decorate the top portion of the cork. A large jewel looks especially nice atop the cork, and your genie will like it too.

Genie Command Ring

After you set genies free from their bottles, silently call them back by lightly rubbing this jeweled ring. But I'll tell you a wizardly secret for making the ring work even better. Create a special ring for each genie, to keep each one at your beck and call.

WHAT YOU NEED

- tinsel stems in silver or gold
- wood dowel or stick about 1/2 inch (1.3 cm) in diameter (optional)
- large plastic jewels or cabochons, round or flat marbles, or large beads
- hot-glue gun and glue sticks (optional)
- scissors

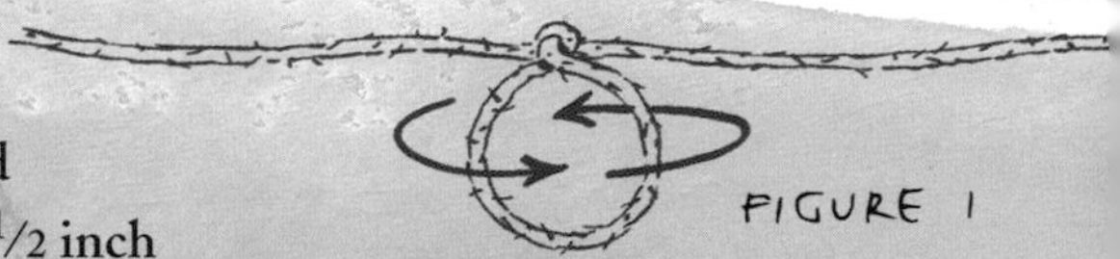

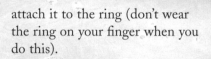

FIGURE 1

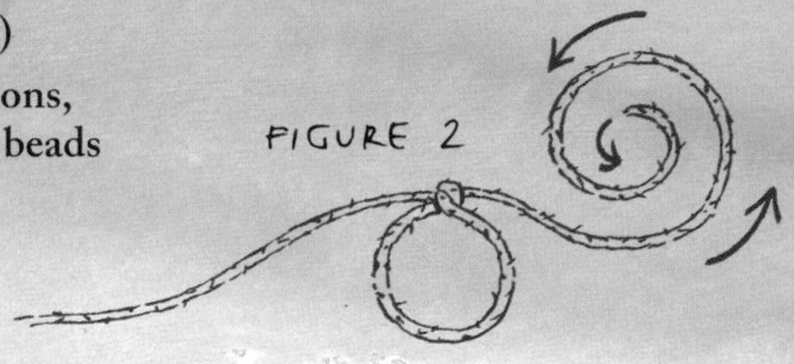

FIGURE 2

INSTRUCTIONS

1. Tightly coil a single tinsel stem around the finger (or thumb!) you want to wear your ring on. You can also wind the coil on a dowel or stick about the same size as your finger.

2. If you like, use more than one stem to form a band. You can twist or braid several stems together to create a thicker ring. Or wrap a stem of one color around a stem of another color.

3. Wrap the band you made in step 2 around your finger or a dowel. Twist it together to form a ring (figure 1). Use a dab of hot glue on the jewel to attach it to the ring (don't wear the ring on your finger when you do this).

4. Wind the loose ends around the stone or in spirals (figure 2), or use the scissors to cut the ends off as you like. If you use beads, thread them on the stem ends of the tinsel, and twist or wind the ends together to secure.

5. If you made a single coil, hot glue the jewel to the coil (not while you're wearing the ring!).

6. Make as many rings as you have genies that you want to summon.

"OPEN, I command!"

Shazaam, ka-blam!

ABRACADABRA, KALAMAZOO!

Aladdin's Tent Game

In many stories about hidden treasures, the hero or heroine has to pass a test or solve a problem to win the prize. In this game, players get into the Desert Wizard's Lair by making up magical words or sentences. Aladdin's Treasure Chest, filled with wrapped prizes, is inside the lair. If you don't summon a genie to be the judge for the game, an adult helper will do.

WHAT YOU NEED

• Desert Wizard's Lair (see page 64)
• Aladdin's Treasure Chest (see page 64)
• small prizes, enough so each guest gets one
• silver and gold wrapping paper
• tape
• adult wizard

HOW TO PLAY

1. After you've made your Desert Wizard's Lair and Aladdin's Treasure Chest, place the chest inside the lair. Wrap all the prizes and put them in the chest. Arrange the coverings over the lair so the entrance is covered by a rug or fabric that has to be pulled aside when someone wants to go in.

2. Have the party guests sit in a semicircle around the entrance, while the adult wizard stands beside the entrance to the lair.

3. The adult wizard should now open the entrance briefly to display the chest and prizes. Explain that each player will take turns coming up with magical commands to convince the adult wizard to let them into the cave. (It gets more difficult as the game proceeds, because players can't repeat what others have said. Let younger players go first.)

4. The more fantastical the words, the better! Funny is good, too. A few examples: *"Abracadabra, kalamazoo! Let me in, why don't you?!!" "Shazaam, ka-blam! Open, I command!" "Genie weenie meanie!"* You get the idea.

5. Prizes are awarded, of course, to everyone who tries! Keep playing until all the prizes are given out.

Reading Palms for Fun

I learned to read palms a few hundred years ago from a dear Gypsy friend of mine, Madame Chovihani (CHO-vuh-HA-nee). The idea is that you can tell your future—and what kind of person you are—from the lines on your hands and fingers. (By the way, did you know that Gypsies may have come from ancient Egypt or India? Maybe that's why they're such good fortunetellers.) Anyway, partygoers should form groups of two and take turns reading each other's palms. See if you and your friends agree about what you "see" in each other's hands!

MARLA BAGGETTA

WHAT YOU NEED

- photocopy of figure 1
- thumbtacks or tape
- teams of two players each

INSTRUCTIONS

1. Make a photocopy of figure 1. Even better, have the copy shop enlarge it so it's big enough to read from a distance. Mount it on the wall.

2. Arrange chairs in groups of two, facing each other. Have someone read steps 3 through 11 out loud. While studying the photocopy, players should take turns reading each other's hands. Take a peek at your own too!

3. If you're right-handed, the left hand shows the future you were born with. The right hand shows how much has come true. (Reverse this for those left-handed.) Deep, clear lines means you can feel both very happy and very sad. Faint lines means you need to get out of your room and live more!

4. Look at the skin and the shape of the hands and fingers. Smooth skin means a person has good manners and lots of energy. Long fingers and hands mean a person is good at art. A broad, square hand says a person is strong and likes to stay busy. Gentle, dreamy people have long fingers. Outdoorsy types have round or flat fingers. Look at the thumb. A long center bone

FIGURE 1

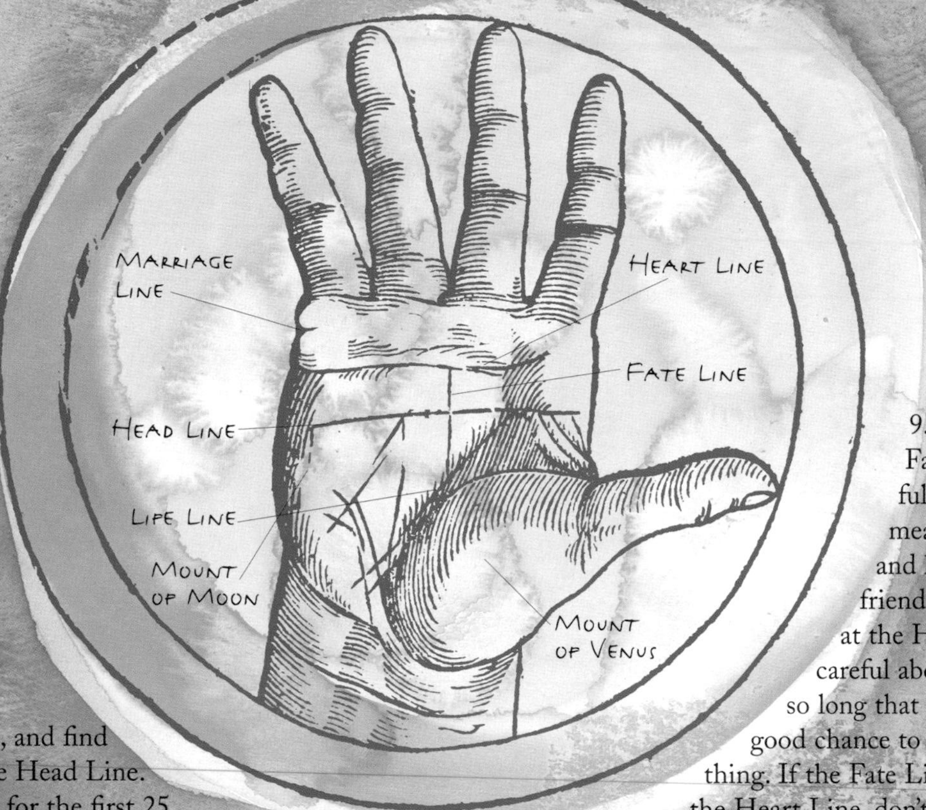

MARRIAGE LINE

HEART LINE

FATE LINE

HEAD LINE

LIFE LINE

MOUNT OF MOON

MOUNT OF VENUS

means a person is good at thinking. A short top bone means they don't have much will power and will often eat an extra cookie!

5. Find the Life Line, and find where it runs near the Head Line. The first third stands for the first 25 years of your life. The next third is the next 25 years. The last third the final part of your life.

6. Find the Mount of Venus. Do you see another line that's closer to it than the Life Line? Does it run the same direction as the Life Line? That's good luck! If the Life Line rides high on your hand, you want to do well in school and games. If the line circles into the palm, you share things with friends.

7. Find the tiny lines that connect the Life and Head lines. See where they touch the Life Line? That tells when you'll reach important goals in your life. If a triangle is formed by the Life Line and two tiny lines, you have a very special talent. Find out what it is, and use it!

8. Compare the Head and Heart lines. If the Head Line is longer, you tend to think a lot. If the Heart Line is longer, you're more of a "feeling" person. A long, deep Head Line means you're really smart! A deep Heart Line means you have deep feelings. A short Heart Line means you'll have lots of boyfriends or girlfriends.

9. Find the Fate Line. A full, deep one means success and lots of friends. If it stops at the Head Line, be careful about thinking so long that you miss a good chance to do something. If the Fate Line breaks at the Heart Line, don't let your feelings get in the way of good luck.

10. Find the Marriage Line. It shows us how many times you'll care so deeply for someone, you'll always remember that person. A full Mount of Venus means you can be a good, kind friend.

11. Find the Mount of the Moon. If it's well developed, you are imaginative and practical. And finally, if lines form a triangle on the Mount of the Moon, you could make a great wizard!

71

Genie Hummus & Toasted Pita Bread

Do you pronounce it "WHO-mus" or "HUM-us?" We'll never know for sure, because hummus was the secret snack of genies before a mortal stole the recipe. Genies are still so mad, they refuse to speak its name! And pita bread is as old as magic in the Middle East.

WHAT YOU NEED

Yield: 2 cups (.48 L)
• 19-ounce can (532 g) of chickpeas
• adult wizard
• food processor or blender
• $^1/_2$ cup (133 mL) toasted sesame oil
• $^1/_4$ cup (66 mL) sesame tahini
• $^1/_4$ cup (66 mL) lemon juice
4 medium garlic cloves
• $^1/_4$ teaspoon (2 g) salt
3 to 4 dashes hot red pepper sauce
• $^1/_4$ cup (66 mL) water
• 4 teaspoons (20 g) fresh mint leaves

INSTRUCTIONS

1. Open the can of chickpeas. Drain and rinse them thoroughly.

2. With an adult wizard's help, put the chickpeas in the food processor. Blend until smooth.

3. Add everything but the water and mint leaves to the mixture. Blend until smooth.

4. Add the water and blend again.

5. Coarsely chop the mint leaves and stir them into the hummus, or garnish the edges of the hummus with the whole leaves. Serve with toasted pita bread.

Toasted Pita Bread

WHAT YOU NEED

- pita bread
- sharp knife or scissors
- baking sheet
- oven

ADULT WIZARD SUPERVISION!

INSTRUCTIONS

1. Preheat the oven to 400°F (204°C).

2. Cut the pita into small triangles. Be sure to divide the pita in half, so each triangle is only one layer of bread.

3. Place the pita onto the baking sheet and toast for 6 minutes, or until golden brown.

Swordplay Shish Kebabs with Dip

It's a little-known fact that Arabian knights were great cooks. Their greatest invention, the shish kebab, happened by accident when a sword fight spilled into a kitchen. Remember, skewer the fruit, not your friends! And no running or flying while eating.

WHAT YOU NEED

Yield: 20 servings
- Assorted fruit, including cantaloupe, melon, strawberries, seedless grapes, and bananas
- kitchen knife
- 20 skewers (cocktail swords preferred)
- medium-size bowl
- 2 tablespoons (30 g) frozen orange or apple juice
- 2 cups (400 g) plain or vanilla yogurt
- pinch of cinnamon

INSTRUCTIONS

1. Cut all the fruit into bite-size pieces.

2. Spear the fruit with the skewers. Cover with plastic wrap and refrigerate.

3. In the bowl, blend the frozen juice concentrate and the yogurt. Garnish the dip with a pinch of cinnamon.

4. Serve the fruit kebabs with the dip.

Oasis Punch

Sometimes magic carpet rides over hot deserts leave me thirsty. I like to get the dust out of my mouth with this sweet, fruity drink.

WHAT YOU NEED

Yield: 18 to 20 servings
- 1 cup (200 g) sugar
- 1 cup (240 mL) water
- medium-size saucepan
- large pitcher

1 42-ounce (190 g) can pineapple juice
- 2 6-ounce (170 g) cans frozen lemonade
- 2 quarts (2 L) ginger ale

INSTRUCTIONS

1. Mix the sugar and water in the saucepan. Bring the mixture to a boil and stir until the sugar dissolves. Remove the mixture from heat.

2. Combine the juice, frozen lemonade, and ginger ale in the large pitcher. Add the sugar syrup and stir well.

3. Cover and refrigerate the punch. Serve it well chilled.

The Legend of Ali Baba and the Forty Thieves

This is the story of a magic cave in old Persia, a young man named Ali Baba, who was a little too greedy for treasure, and smart servant girl who uses her head!

Ali Baba gathered wood to earn a living. One day, as he w loading his mules, Ali Baba saw dust clouds rise in the distance A band of robbers was riding toward him! Ali Baba hid his animals and climbed a tree.

The men stopped near Ali Baba's hiding place, dismounted, and began unloading their horses. Shaking from fright, Ali Baba counted forty men i all. Their leader faced a large rock and said, "Open, Sesame!" To Ali Baba's amazement, the rock moved aside, revealing a secret doorway. The robbers took their booty inside and came out a short time later. While mounting h horse, the leader said, "Shut, Sesame!" The rock slid back into place, sealing the cave. The bandits galloped away.

Ali Baba climbed from the tree and crept over to the mysterious rock. H didn't know if the head thief was a magician or if the rock was charmed. There was only one way to find out. "Open, Sesame!" said Ali Baba. To his delight, the rock obeyed Ali Baba's command.

The robbers' lair amazed Ali Baba. There were huge piles of gold and si ver coins and many brightly colored silks. There were carpets and chests fu of jewels. Ali Baba had never seen such treasures. He loaded as much as he could onto his mules, then commanded the rock, "Shut, Sesame!" When he arrived home he and his wife immediately buried the treasure.

Ali Baba returned to the cave many times, taking small portions of the stolen riches, so the thieves wouldn't notice. Soon he had a fortune and beg to live like a rich man, buying new land and new clothes.

Finally the robbers noticed how much treasure was missing and started looking for the culprit. Their leader disguised himself as a traveling oil merchant and went into the city to ask if anyone nearby had suddenly become rich. The tailor told him that Ali Baba, who had been poor for so long, had been buying many fine suits. He directed the thief to Ali Baba's fine new home. Later that night, the thief visited Ali Baba and asked for shelter for the night. Ali Baba agreed, not recognizing him. The leader placed large jars in Ali Baba's barn and ordered his men to hide in them with their weapons.

That night, Ali Baba's servant, Akilah, noticed that they'd run out of oil for the house lamps. She went to the barn to get more oil and spied the men waiting to ambush the house. Luckily for Ali Baba, Akilah was true to her name (akilah means "intelligent" in Arabic). She crept into the house, boiled a big pot of oil, and carried it to the barn. She poured oil into each jar. Smarting from the hot oil, the men dropped their weapons and fled. Their leader fled with his band too, never to be heard from again.

For a long time, Ali Baba didn't go back to the thieves' stronghold outside the city. When he did, everything was exactly as the thieves had left it, and Ali Baba and his family remained one of the wealthiest and best-known families in their village for many generations to come.

Welcome Springtime Fairy Frolic

Fairies love to give and attend parties with lots of dancing, good food, and drink. I always say yes when they invite me, even if I have to do a Shrinking Charm on myself to fit in. Here's how to create a charming spring celebration to enchant every Little Person you know.

Party Decorations

Most fairies feel at home near trees and flowers, so pick a good day in the weather forecast and have your party in your backyard, patio, or garden. This makes decorating easy too.

Fairies love the colors red, blue, green, and white. Cover the banquet table with a colored tablecloth or crepe paper. Tape matching paper, silk, or cut flowers around the edge of the table and any chairs. Make a centerpiece of your Decorated Beastie Eggs (page 81), and set small saucers of the dye ingredients around the centerpiece. During the party, the guests can play a Color Divination Game by guessing which ingredient produced which color on the eggs. Give prizes— or at least a flower—to everyone!

Set vases and pots of fairy-friendly flowers and herbs around the party area. You can also make fairy circles for each table by arranging 3-inch pots of red and white flowers in a circle in the middle. That way, invisible fairy guests will have safe places to party without getting squashed. *Impatiens wallerana* is a good choice, and you can give the flowers to guests or plant them after the party.

Your most important party decoration will be a good, old-fashioned maypole. The point is for everyone to dance around the pole while they hold the ends of the ribbons, which weave together in a pattern. It's fun, even if you get tangled up! Guests can make Jack o' the Woods Masks, Fairy Wristlets, and Fairy Wings, and wear them while they dance (see pages 82 through 84).

ANGELICA

Good Magic Flower Power Robe

Extra-big images of "good magic" flowers and herbs give this party robe posy power! Try wearing it when you go outside to water your baby mandrakes too. Just remember, fairies love flowers, so when you wear this robe you may sense the fluttering of their wings. If you feel an itch or a tickle, move gently so you don't flatten a fairy!

WHAT YOU NEED

- Basic Robe on page 135, made of light-colored fabric
- herb and flower patterns of your choice
- colored markers or pencils
- iron (optional)
- silk flowers (optional)
- needle and thread or hot glue gun and glue sticks (optional)

ROSEMARY

THYME

MOONFLOWER

PERIWINKLE

INSTRUCTIONS

1. After making the Basic Robe, choose the herb and flower patterns you like. Take them to a photocopy shop and have them enlarge the patterns.

2. Use the colored markers or pencils to add color to the photocopies.

3. Take the photocopies back to the copy shop and have them create iron-on transfers from the photocopies.

4. At this point, you can either iron the transfers onto the robe, or have the copy shop heat-set the transfers to the robe.

5. If desired, cut off the stems of the silk flowers. Hot glue or sew them to the robe. Place a posy here and there, or go wild and attach them to the cuffs, hem, and neckline.

Angelica   If you want a plant with the strongest good magic, choose angelica. It's said to bloom on the May feast day of Saint Michael the Archangel. Tradition says every part of it protects against evil, especially the root.

Thyme   Bees love thyme, as well as fairies. This herb has tiny, very fragrant leaves and masses of little lilac flowers.

Periwinkle ❀ This low-growing flower has dark green leaves and white, deep purple, or blue blossoms with five petals that grow in a pinwheel shape. Evil spirits can't stand it.

Moonflower ❀ The moon is so important in stories of magic, it's fitting for a wizard or sorceress to have a picture of its namesake! The gorgeous white flower closes during the day, then opens up as big as a salad plate at night, giving off a heavenly smell like cloves.

Rosemary ❀ Fairies love rosemary. It has tiny, lavender-colored flowers and small evergreen needles that smell good.

Merry Maypole

Even the most dignified wizards love to caper around a maypole, robes and ribbons flying! In the old days in England, villagers crowned a May Queen. Then they put a tree trunk on the village green and decorated it with ropes of flowers and leaves. Sometimes Jack o' the Woods (page 84) showed up too. These directions are for a maypole that can accommodate 14 dancers. Adjust the number of ribbons as needed. If you have an odd number of party guests, let an adult wizard play too! See page 85 for a special maypole song and dance.

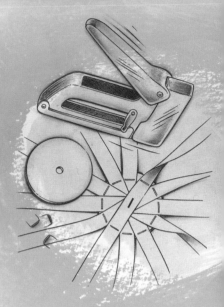

WHAT YOU NEED

- 10-foot (3 m) wooden pole, 1½ to 2 inches (3.8 to 5 cm) in diameter
- wooden finial in decorative shape
- 2 wooden disks, 8 inches (20.3 cm) in diameter
- paint with gloss finish in color of your choice
- paintbrush
- power drill and bit with a diameter to match the screw (see below)
- 7 rolls of 1-inch (2.5 cm) satin ribbon, 10 yards (9 m) each, in bright, fairy-friendly colors
- scissors
- hot-glue gun and glue sticks
- staple gun
- 1 double-ended screw, 3 inches (7.6 cm) long
- silk flowers or fresh cut flowers (optional)
- patio umbrella stand
- metal U-pins
- mallet

INSTRUCTIONS

1. Paint the pole, finial, and disks and let dry.

2. Drill a hole in the center of one end of the pole and in the centers of the two disks.

3. Stretch out the ribbons. Fold each ribbon in half at its midpoint, and cut a small hole on the fold. Unfold the ribbon.

4. Set one of the wooden disks on a flat work surface. Arrange the ribbons on top of the disk like evenly spaced spokes of a wheel, with the holes you cut in the ribbons positioned over the hole drilled in the disk. You should end up with 14 "free" ends of ribbon for the dancers. When you've arranged the ribbons to your liking, tack them in place with the hot glue. Staple the ribbons in place, too, inside the rim of the disk.

5. Fix one end of the 3-inch (7.6 cm) screw in the hole you drilled in the pole. Slide the ribbon-decorated disk over the screw so the ribbons are facing up. Slide the second disk on top to make a "sandwich."

6. Center the finial over the protruding screw, and screw it on.

7. Hot glue the flowers to the finial and disk if desired.

8. Insert the pole in the umbrella stand, and secure it to the ground with the U-pins, using the mallet to drive them into the ground.

Decorated Beastie Egg Centerpiece

ADULT WIZARD SUPERVISION!

The egg is a symbol of spring, and many magical animals lay eggs, you know. But if you don't feel like fighting a bad-tempered beast for its eggs today, you can make your own from grocery-store eggs, veggies, and fruits.

WHAT YOU NEED

- raw eggs with white shells
- adult wizard

HOT DYE INGREDIENTS
(and the colors they create):
- 4 cups (800 g) of chopped beets (deep pink)
- 4 cups (800 g) of fresh or frozen blueberries (rich lavender)
- brewed coffee (deep brown)
- skins from 12 onions, about 4 cups (800 g) firmly packed (orangey brown)
- 3 tablespoons (45 g) turmeric spice (bright gold)

COLD DYE INGREDIENTS
(and the colors they create):
- 2 heads of red cabbage (blue)
- 12-ounce (330 g) package of fresh cranberries (pale pink)
- adult wizard
- large cook pot
- water
- measuring cup or pitcher
- tablespoon
- white vinegar (quantity depends on how much water you use; see steps 1 and 5)
- large, perforated spoon
- paper towels
- empty egg carton
- strainer
- large saucepan
- glass dishes or paper cups
- twine, rubber bands (optional)
- large basket or bowl

INSTRUCTIONS

1. First you'll boil the eggs. With the help of an adult wizard, put them in one layer in the cook pot and cover with cold water about 1 inch (2.5 cm) above the eggs. Measure the water as you add it, then mix in 2 tablespoons (30 mL) of vinegar for every quart of water in the pot.

2. You can color eggs with hot or cold dyes. When using a hot-dye ingredient, the eggs color as you cook them. Go ahead and add whatever color ingredient you want. Bring everything to a boil, then turn down the heat and simmer the eggs 30 minutes. Let cool.

3. Use the paper towels to cover your work surface. Set the open egg carton on top, then use the perforated spoon to remove the eggs from the pot to the empty egg carton. Let dry.

4. To color eggs with a cold dye, follow step 1, bringing the eggs to a boil, then turn the heat down and simmer them 10 minutes. Turn off the heat, transfer the eggs to the strainer, and let cool.

5. Add the cold-dye color ingredient to 2 quarts (2.2 L) of water in the saucepan. Mix in 6 tablespoons (90 mL) of the vinegar, then add the dye ingredient. Bring to a boil and cook until the water is a rich color. Let cool.

6. Strain the cold dye, then put enough cooled liquid to cover an egg into a glass dish or paper cup.

7. Put a cold, hard-boiled egg into the

continued

dye. The longer it soaks, the richer the color will be (especially for red cabbage dye). Dip your egg in briefly to make it pale blue, or soak it overnight for a rich blue fit for a king!

8. Try layering colors. If you want chartreuse green eggs (like a dragon's), boil the eggs in a turmeric hot dye. Let cool, then put them in a cold dye made from red cabbage.

9. To make a two-color egg, color it with hot dye and let cool. Fill a dish with enough cold dye to cover the egg halfway; let it sit. Wrap parts of a white or previously dyed egg with rubber bands before hot- or cold-dyeing it; the covered parts will keep their original color.

10. Arrange the dry eggs in the basket.

Fairy Wristlet

You can lure fairies to come out of hiding and play when you wear these magical wrist charms. They're just like the wristlets fairies wear. There's not a fairy alive who won't be tempted to appear when they hear tiny, tinkling sounds and see ribbons flittering about in the air. They'll think other fairies are having a party without them and come peeking about. They're like that, you know.

WHAT YOU NEED

- chenille stems in bright colors, about 12 inches (30.5 cm) long, 2 stems per wristlet
- small jingle bells (the smaller the better)
- ribbon, 1/4 inch (6 mm) wide
- scissors
- large pony beads
- tiny silk flowers (optional)
- hot-glue gun and glue sticks (optional)

INSTRUCTIONS

1. Measure and cut lengths of ribbon 12 inches (30.5 cm) long or longer if desired. You'll need several lengths for each wristlet.

2. Twist the two chenille stems together at one end.

3. Thread several pony beads on both stems, pushing them to the twist. Twist the stems together to secure them.

4. Make another twist about 1/2 inch (1.3 cm) from the last. Tie a length of ribbon next to the twist on one of the stems. Twist the stems again to secure the ribbon.

5. Repeat the previous step, adding a jingle bell.

6. Alternate pony beads, ribbons, and jingle bells along the length of each stem.

7. When you have filled the stems with bells and ribbons, twist the ends to secure the decorations. If desired, hot glue the tiny silk blossoms along the stems.

8. Wind the chenille stems around your wrist or ankle. You can also twist the ends together to make a slip-on bangle.

Fairy Wings & Wand

What's a fairy without wings and a wand? A leprechaun, of course. But some fairies have little wands and large, glittery wings. Other fairies have long wands and tiny wings. Some fairies store their wings in the closet, but whenever they take them out, they get bigger and brighter. What kind of fairy are you? Make wings and wands for your guests, or set up a make-your-own craft area. The more fairies, the merrier!

WHAT YOU NEED FOR WINGS

- wing template on this page
- wing materials such as translucent vellum, construction paper, felt, colored foam, recycled plastic milk jugs, or cardboard (for really BIG wings)
- scissors or craft knife
- pencil
- glitter, acrylic paint, markers, sequins, or tinsel rope (optional)
- safety pins or self-adhesive brooch pin backs*

*available in the beading area of craft or bead stores

FLAT WINGS

1. Photocopy the wing template (fig. 1), enlarging or shrinking it to make wings the size you want. Use the scissors to cut out the template. Set it aside.

2. Fold the vellum or other material in half. Lay half of the template on the folded line and trace around it with a pencil. If you're using heavy cardboard, place the whole template on the cardboard and trace around it. Cut out the wings, but don't cut down the folded line!

3. Use the paints, glitter, sequins, and tinsel to decorate the wings. Sketch feathers or curlicues on them!

4. Using the safety pins or pin backs, attach the wings to your clothing slightly below the base of the neck. If you're making really big wings, you'll need several safety pins!

DIMENSIONAL WINGS

1. Repeat step 1 of the directions for Flat Wings.

2. Tape the wing template to the corner of a plastic milk jug, and tape it to each side. Trace around the template.

3. Use the scissors to cut out the joined wings, then decorate both sides of each wing. Attach to clothing as described in step 4.

WHAT YOU NEED FOR A WAND

- Basic Wand on page 138
- additional decoration, such as glitter, ribbons, feathers, jingle bells, sequins, copper or brass wire, or tinsel stems
- pencil (optional)

INSTRUCTIONS

1. When selecting your twig or dowel, the fairy rule of thumb is "no longer than your forearm."

TEMPLATE FOR FAIRY WINGS

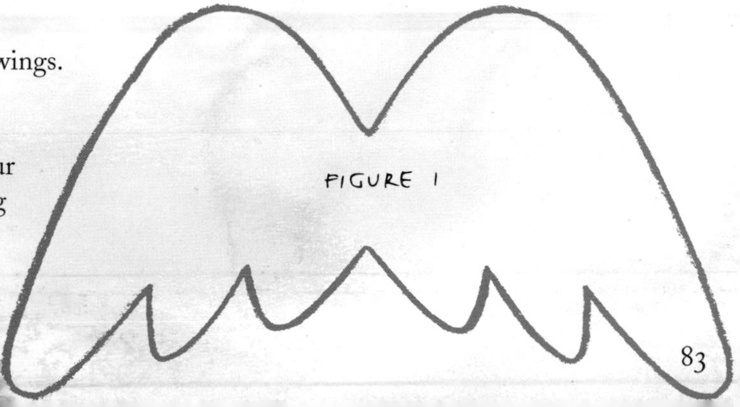

FIGURE 1

continued

2. Follow steps 2, 5, and 6 of the Basic Wand instructions on page 138. (Remove the wand topper before you paint the wand.)

3. You can decorate your wand topper any number of ways. Paint it with a base color, then add designs in another color. Coat it with white glue and roll it in glitter. Let dry.

4. If desired, cut four lengths of ribbon. Arrange them on the tip of the wand in a pattern like spokes on a wheel. Use a small dot of hot glue to glue each ribbon to the tip. Tie a jingle bell (or a feather!) to the ribbon ends.

5. Hot glue the wand topper to the wand. To give your wand extra power, add Dragon Heartstring Coils by following steps 1, 2, and 7 in the Basic Wand instructions.

Jack O' the Woods Mask

If you go for a walk in the woods and you spy a green, horned man with a mask of oak leaves covering his face, you've seen Jack-in-the-Green. He's also called Jack O' the Woods and he's the spirit of trees, plants, and foliage. Jack makes rain, too, so I hope you brought your umbrella!

WHAT YOU NEED

- mask and leaf templates on this page
- thin card stock (file folder or poster board)
- stapler or tape
- scissors
- construction papers, handmade papers, or other decorative papers in shades of green, gold, yellow, orange, or brown
- white craft glue
- 2 yards (1.8 m) ribbon
- real oak leaves (optional)

INSTRUCTIONS

1. Use a photocopier to enlarge the mask template to fit your face. Staple or tape the pattern to the card stock.

2. Use the scissors to cut out the mask and the eye holes.

3. Make small holes that are level with the eye holes on either side of the mask.

ENLARGE THIS MASK TO FIT YOUR FACE

USE THIS TEMPLATE OF A REAL OAK LEAF

A Maypole Song and Dance

Your guests can dance, skip, or run around the maypole, singing and jingling their Fairy Wristlets (page 82) in time to the music. Here's how to wrap (and unwrap) ribbons around the pole, and a song with a very familiar tune. To help guests learn the dance, copy the diagram on a large piece of poster board. If anyone gets tangled up, just stop and correct it. The point is to have fun.

4. Use a photocopier to make bigger, smaller, and same-size copies of the leaf template. Make several copies! You'll want lots of leaves to decorate the mask. Tape or staple the leaf patterns to the construction paper or decorative papers. Cut out the leaves.

5. Fold each leaf in half lengthwise and crease it with your fingernail. Open the leaf back up.

6. Arrange the leaves on your mask. Try arranging them in different ways. When you're happy with the way they look, glue them to the mask.

7. Cut the ribbon into two equal pieces. Fold a length in half, slip the folded end through one of the small holes, and bring the ends through the loop. Tighten the loop carefully so you don't tear the mask. Repeat on the other side.

WEAVING A GRAND PLAIT (translation: "Big Braid")

INSTRUCTIONS

1. Put on some music, or practice singing the song below. Have all the dancers stand in A/B, A/B pairs, with A on the right and B on the left, facing each other. It's not necessary to pair up boy/girl.

2. On the signal of an adult wizard, everyone starts singing and moving at the same time, alternating the sides they pass on: first the right shoulder, then the left.

3. After the ribbons have been braided around part of the pole, the adult wizard gives another signal and the dancers reverse direction.

WIZARD'S MAYPOLE SONG

Wizards can sing this song to the tune of "She'll Be Comin' Round the Mountain When She Comes".

Wizards dancing round the maypole
when May comes
Wizards dancing round the maypole
when May comes
Wizards dancing round the maypole
Wizards dancing round the maypole
Wizards dancing round the maypole
when May comes

A

B

Fairies, Flowers, and Fortune-Telling

Fairies love flowers, herbs, and other green living things. If you visit a garden or a forest, you just might see a fairy. But you have to wait and be very quiet. In Italy, people say that if you watch a rosemary bush very carefully, you may see a fairy creep out from underneath. If you can make friends with him, he'll teach you how to change your shape into something else. Think about what animal or tree you'd like to be, in case this ever happens to you. Fairies also like the herb called thyme, so plant some in your garden. It smells good too. The rose is the fairies' favorite flower, and they protect the beautiful blooms. Even if you can't see a Little Person around, it might be best to ask if it's okay before you pick a rose.

Have you found a ring of red-and-white mushrooms or flowers growing in a circle in your yard or in the woods? You're in luck, you've found a fairy ring! The ring is a spot where fairies meet to dance and sing at night. If you find a ring, stand in the middle when the moon is full and make a wish. Legend says it will come true. Sometimes winged fairies change how they look when they fly, to look like dandelion fluff or butterflies. Before you blow on a dandelion head to help the fairies fly away, ask a question with a "yes" or "no" answer. If the answer is yes, all the fluff will fly off the stem. If the answer is no, well, try again.

Did you know you can use flowers to tell the future? (I think a fairy must have taught a wizard how to do it.) Here's how it works. Go into your garden or a meadow or an empty lot where wildflowers are growing. Without looking (don't cheat!), pick any petal off a flower.

Now look at the petal. If it has four lines in it, something good is about to happen to you. If there are thick lines that curve to the right, money is coming your way.

If the lines go to the left, be careful not to get in trouble over the next few days (so stop teasing your little brother!). If the flower petal has streaks of a different color in it, count them. Eight or nine streaks means you'll have lots of boyfriends or girlfriends, while seven means you tend to stick with a few really good, loyal friends. If you count 11 streaks, you're going to change your mind or get rid of a bad habit very soon.

Mandrake Cupcakes

Do you have mandrakes in your garden? If you do, you know that it takes a while for them to develop their heads, arms, and legs. These cupcakes contain very young mandrakes that partygoers can harvest themselves. You might want to hand out earplugs to anyone who fears the magic root's deathly scream.

WHAT YOU NEED

- 1 box chocolate cake mix and the ingredients specified on the box
- candied orange slices
- cupcake liners
- muffin tin
- chocolate frosting

INSTRUCTIONS

1. Prepare the cake mix as directed and preheat the oven to the specified heat.

2. Slice a triangular-shaped wedge out of each orange slice to give them little legs.

3. Put the cupcake wrappers into the muffin tin. Fill them about halfway with the cupcake batter.

4. Gently press an orange slice into the center of each cupcake. Smooth out the batter. Repeat for each cupcake.

5. Bake for 19 to 22 minutes, or until a toothpick inserted in the middle comes out clean.

6. Cool for 15 minutes, then frost with the chocolate frosting.

Lavender Lemonade

Titania (tie-TAY-NEE-ah), Queen of the Fairies, serves this lemonade every year at her Spring Ball. I've heard that when all the supernatural guests waltz, spring flowers bloom wherever their feet touch the earth.

WHAT YOU NEED

Yield: 6 servings
- saucepan
- 5 cups (1200 mL) water
- $1/2$ cup (112 grams) lavender blooms, stemmed
- fine mesh sieve
- $1/3$ cup (800 mL) freshly squeezed lemon juice
- $1/2$ cup (100 grams) sugar
- mint leaves
- lavender sprigs

INSTRUCTIONS

1. In a small saucepan, bring the water to a rolling boil. Remove from heat and add the lavender blooms. Cover and steep for 10 minutes.

2. Strain the mixture through a fine mesh sieve. Set the tea aside.

3. Add the lemon juice and sugar to the lavender tea. Refrigrate until chilled.

4. Garnish the tea with mint leaves and lavender sprigs before serving.

Candied Violets
and Rose Petal Candy

Fairies like sweet things, and candied flowers are a special treat for us wizards, too. But be careful. You'll smell like a fairy if you eat too many, and they might decide to whisk you away to Fairyland for a few hundred years.

Candied Violets

WHAT YOU NEED

- violet blossoms
- handheld mixer
- 1 egg white
- waxed paper
- cookie sheet
- granulated sugar

INSTRUCTIONS

1. Gather your violets. Wash the flowers gently in cool water, and set them aside to drip dry.

2. Use the handheld mixer to whip the egg white until it's frothy but doesn't form peaks. Tip: the bowl and beaters should be absolutely dry before you start.

3. Lay a piece of waxed paper on the cookie sheet. Dip the violets one by one into the egg white, roll them lightly in the sugar, and place on the waxed paper. Let them dry for a day.

Rose Petal Candy

WHAT YOU NEED

- 2 ounces gum arabic*
- $^1/_2$ pint (1 L) water
- fresh rose petals
- cookie sheet
- 1 pound (448 g) sugar
- $^1/_2$ pint (1 L) water
- red food coloring

*found in candymaking supply departments

INSTRUCTIONS

1. Dissolve the gum arabic in $^1/_2$ pint (1 L) of water. Put the rose petals on the cookie sheet and sprinkle them with the water and a little sugar.

2. Dry the rose petals for 24 hours, then place them on a heat-resistant plate.

3. Boil $^1/_2$ pint (1 L) of water and add the sugar. Continue to boil until the sugar dissolves and threads off the spoon.

4. Add a few drops of the red food coloring to the sugar mixture.

5. Pour this mixture over the rose petals. Dry for another 24 hours, then place the rose candy in a warm oven to finish drying.

THE STORY OF
Tamlin, Andreana, &
THE FAIRY QUEEN

If you met your true love (or someone you really, really liked!), would you be brave enough to rescue him from a wicked fairy's spell? Once upon a time, a girl named Andreana (Ahn-dree-AH-na) happened upon a fairy well. Fairies are enchanted creatures who bring luck, both the good kind and the bad kind. Only the fairy can decide which it will be.

Young Andreana had never seen a fairy. But she was true to her name, which means "brave girl." "If I'm very careful," thought Andreana, "I can peek into the well and see what there is to see, and no harm will come to me." She crept near the well, crouching beside a rosebush (fairies like roses, you know). Glancing around, she plucked a flower and put it in her hair. Seeing no one, Andreana knelt on the stones on the edge of the well. She peered in but saw only her reflection in the water below. Disappointed, she rose to leave.

To her surprise, a boy appeared from nowhere. Dressed all in green, he sat astride a horse. "When you pick a flower from my rosebush, you call me," he said, swinging down from the horse. "I am Tamlin, a knight of the Queen of Elfland."

"I am —," she began, before stopping suddenly. Andreana realized she was face to face with a fairy. And she could not tell if he was good or bad.

Tamlin read the concern on her face. "I won't hurt you. I once was a mortal, like you. I tripped on a fairy hill and was kidnapped by the Queen. She has put me under her spell. It's been so long since I've talked to anyone mortal, please tell me your name and stay awhile," he said. Trusting him, Andreana introduced herself. They talked until night fell and it was time for Andreana to go home.

She returned a few days later, plucked a rose, and Tamlin appeared again. Soon, they met every day, and fell in love. But a mortal and a fairy can never marry.

"There must be a way to break the Queen's spell," Andreana said.

"I've heard of one way, but I think it takes more courage and strength than any girl has," Tamlin said woefully.

"Tell me what to do," Andreana said, "and I will do it."

On the full moon, at the stroke of midnight, the fairy Queen rides with all her fairy knights. If Andreana could knock Tamlin from his horse and hold onto him tight, the spell would be broken. But the Queen would use magic to try to foil Andreana. She would turn Tamlin into all kinds of wild beasts before finally making him into a burning chunk of coal. At the moment Tamlin became the coal, Andreana must toss him in the well.

At the next full moon, Andreana was ready. As the Queen rode past, Andreana spied Tamlin. She rushed out of her hiding place, pulled him from his horse, and jumped on his back. The Queen looked back. Tamlin turned into a slippery snake with a long, spiked tongue. Andreana coiled herself around it. The snake became a wolf with long, sharp teeth. Andreana grabbed its fur and held fast. The wolf became a huge bear with razor-sharp claws. Andreana locked her arms around its neck and her legs around its back. The bear became a lion with a fierce roar. Andreana dug her fingers into its thick mane and held on. Finally, the lion became a fiery piece of coal. Andreana threw it into the well.

Out climbed Tamlin, sopping wet but mortal again. Andreana smiled while the Queen frowned. Too tired to cast more spells, the Queen promised to return and recapture Tamlin. But by then, Tamlin and Andreana had moved far away from the fairy well and lived happily together for the rest of their lives.

EGYPTIAN
Summer Solstice Party

Egyptian sorcerers gave wild parties back in the old days: all the date juice you could drink, palm trees bursting into fireworks, and wizards busy turning each other into camels! They had their biggest parties on the summer solstice (SOUL-stiss), the longest day of the year. Here's how to craft your own sun celebration.

Party Decorations

Ancient Egyptian magic was so strong, it's what we still picture when we think of Egypt: the dark secrets of the pyramids; strange writing in curious hieroglyphs; gods and goddesses with the heads of animals; and fortune-tellers everywhere! The sun was very important to the Egyptians, so hold your party outside on a sunny day.

Copy the hieroglyphs on page 95 by hand (use gold gel pens on black paper) and hang them up. You can also take them to a copy shop (better yet, an architectural blueprint service) and have them blown up really, really big. When dusk comes, replace a few lightbulbs with yellow party bulbs.

Make pyramids of all sizes out of cardboard (see the pattern on page 98). Place them around the party area and hang some up. Arrange them in a formal pattern on your banquet table, and thrill your party guests by telling them it's Karnak, the center of magic and wizardry in old Egypt. You should also have piles of sugar cubes and bowls of icing ready for guests to make their own Sugar Cube Pyramids (page 97) to take home.

Gather empty boxes, baskets, and any other junk you've been meaning to throw out. Spray everything with gold paint. Let dry, and make piles of "Pharaoh's treasure." Collect grasses, reed, or cane from a local riverbank or ditch. Tie them together in swags with a bit of raffia or twine, spray-paint them gold, and tell guests they're magic bulrushes from the River Nile.

This is a great party for young wizards to practice their alchemy and fortune-telling skills. The Egyptians were good at both. Set up tables for potion brewing, Egyptian Dice, and the Yes/No Pendulum Game (pages 101-103). Then get ready for the powers of the Great Beyond to speak!

Egyptian Sorcerer's Tunic

Why in the name of Ra the Sun God would an Egyptian wizard wear a long-sleeved robe at the summer solstice? It's too hot! A sleeveless tunic sewn from lightweight cotton was a much better choice. The tunics were usually plain, because the Egyptians wore so much jewelry. But since this tunic is for a party, use the lotus flower design (an ancient symbol of creation) to decorate yours.

MAKING THE TUNIC

WHAT YOU NEED

- Basic Robe on page 135
- thin cotton fabric
- fabric paints (optional)
- paintbrush (optional)

INSTRUCTIONS

1. In step 1 of the basic instructions, measure the width of the shoulders rather than measuring from wrist to wrist. Add 6 inches (15.2 cm) to the width of your shoulders. For a shorter tunic, measure only from the knee to the shoulder instead of from the shoulder to the floor.

2. In step 2, divide the shoulder width measurement by 2. Measure and mark this measurement from the folded edge.

3. Skip step 5.

4. In step 6 draw the line from the open edge at the bottom of the fabric to the mark you made in step 2 for the shoulder width.

5. Cut the fabric as directed. Open up the robe.

6. Starting at the hem, sew the side seams to approximately 12 inches (30.5 cm) from the folded shoulder line.

7. If desired, decorate only the bottom hem of the robe with a row of lotus flowers and seed pods in the colors of your choice. The Egyptians were especially fond of red and blue.

TEMPLATES FOR THE LOTUS FLOWER DESIGN

ADULT WIZARD SUPERVISION!

WHAT YOU NEED (decorating the tunic)

- **lotus flower and pod templates on this page**
- **scissors**
- **large baking potato**
- **pencil**
- **table knife or craft knife**
- **paper towels**
- **acrylic fabric paints**
- **disposable plate**
- **foam brush**
- **small paintbrush**
- **newspaper**

INSTRUCTIONS

1. Photocopy the lotus flower and pod designs, enlarging or reducing them to "fit" the length and width of the potato.

2. Use the scissors to cut out the designs.

3. Cut the potato in half. Lay the lotus design on the potato. Trace around the design with a pencil.

4. Use the knife tip to trace around the design, pressing the knife about 1/4 inch (6 mm) into the potato.

continued

5. Carve away the potato outside of the cut line, leaving a raised lotus design.

6. Repeat steps 4 and 5 with the remaining potato half and the pod design.

7. Pat the potatoes with the paper towels to get rid of excess moisture.

8. Read and follow the tips for decorating fabric with paint on page 137. Pour fabric paint onto the disposable plate. Use the foam brush to pick up some of the paint and lightly paint the raised lotus.

9. Make a test print on the newspaper. Do you need to use more or less paint on the potato stamp? When you know how much paint is enough, alternate stamping the lotus flower and lotus pod designs onto the hem of the tunic. Let dry.

10. Use the small paintbrush to paint a curved line linking the lotus flower and pod designs. Let dry.

11. Follow the manufacturer's instructions to set the fabric paint.

Egyptian Collar

A fancy metal collar was a well-known mark of power in ancient Egypt. Only the rich and powerful could afford a gold or silver collar with beads, enamels, or embossing. King Tut, Cleopatra, and the wise scientist Ptolemy (TALL-uh-mee) wore them. You can too! Choose symbols from pages 93 and 95 to decorate your collar, or use the hieroglyphic alphabet to personalize it with your name.

WHAT YOU NEED

(for the Collar)

• T-shirt
• newspaper
• pencil
• ruler
• oven liner
• scissors
• metal spoon
• hole punch
• 1 yard (91.4 cm) small ribbon or cord

For Decorating the Collar

• Egyptian images on pages 93 and 95
• abrasive kitchen scrubber
• acrylic paints or dimensional paints*
• paintbrush
• ball-point pen*
• stack of newspapers or magazines
• permanent markers*
• plastic or glass marble jewels, or sequins*
• hot-glue gun and glue sticks

*Use any or all of these to decorate your collar.

INSTRUCTIONS

1. Lay your T-shirt front side up on a flat surface. Smooth out any wrinkles. Cover the shirt with an unfolded sheet of newspaper. You should still be able to feel the neckline with your fingers. Move the paper so that the neckline is just about centered under your paper.

2. Use the pencil to trace the bottom part of the curved neckline onto the newspaper. Feel for the shoulder lines, and use the pencil to trace them onto the newspaper. Remove the shirt from under the paper and set it aside.

3. Use the ruler and pencil to make marks on the newspaper 4 to 5 inches (10.2 to 12.7 cm) from the curved neckline. Connect the marks to make a curved line that crosses both sides of the marked shoulder lines. Let this line cross the shoulder line and extend about 5 inches (12.7 cm).

4. Extend the neckline from the shoulder line to match what you drew in step 5. You should see a fat U-shape. Use the scissors to cut it out.

5. Try on the pattern, wrapping the long ends over your shoulders. You want the long ends to go over the shoulders just a little bit. Trim the pattern as needed.

6. Lay the pattern on the oven liner and trace around the pattern. Cut out the marked pattern with the scissors.

7. Lay the liner cutout on a flat surface. Use the back of the spoon to smooth out any preprinted patterns on the liner.

8. Carefully fold up all edges of the metal $1/4$ inch (6mm) or less. Press the folded edges down with the back of the spoon. The fold will protect you from any sharp edges.

9. Use the punch to make a hole at the back of the inner neck edge on both sides.

10. Cut the length of ribbon or cord in half. Fold one length in half and thread the doubled end through one of the holes. Pull the loose ends through the loop and tighten. Repeat with the other length of ribbon. Use these ribbons to tie the breastplate behind the neck.

11. You can decorate the collar in many different ways, using any of the Egyptian designs. If you use paint to imitate enameled surfaces, use the abrasive kitchen pad to scour the surface of the metal first. This gives the metal "tooth" and helps the paint adhere. Follow the directions for the Celtic Cuff on page 111 to emboss motifs, and hot glue the jewels to the collar as desired.

Some of the HIEROGLYPHIC Alphabet

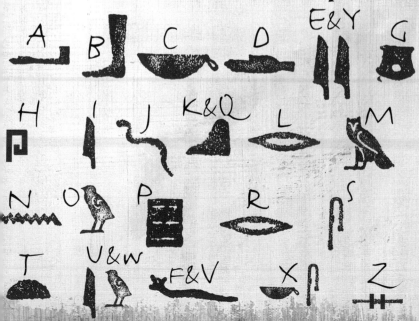

THE SCARAB BEETLE WAS A SACRED SYMBOL TO THE ANCIENT EGYPTIANS.

Egyptian Staff with Anubis Head

THE EYE OF HORUS

Many Egyptian wizards decorated their staffs with animal-headed gods. The results were just what you'd expect! Staffs topped with the jackal head of Anubis (ah-NOO-biss) howled at every full moon or solar eclipse. Falcon-headed Horus (HO-russ) staffs shrieked whenever they saw a mouse. And you can just imagine what a staff with Sebek (SO-beck), the crocodile god, must have done when it was feeling frisky! You can make your own Anubis head by following these directions.

FIGURE 1

WHAT YOU NEED

- Basic Wizard's Staff on page 139
- Anubis head template on opposite page *
- tracing paper
- pencil
- scissors
- black fine-tip permanent marker
- 1 block of floral foam**
- table knife
- polystyrene foam egg**
- hot-glue gun and glue stick**
- toothpicks
- newspaper or tissue paper
- plastic sheeting
- white craft glue
- small bowl
- plastic wrap
- gesso or acrylic primer**
- acrylic paint in gold or other colors
- paintbrushes

*If you want to make a different head, carve the foam base to match one of the other shapes shown in pictures of the other gods. After you've covered it with paper mache, add beaks, teeth, or headdress.
**sold in craft stores

INSTRUCTIONS

1. Use the tracing paper and pencil to copy the side view template of the Anubis head, and cut it out. Place the head template on the floral foam block, and trace around it with the marker.

2. Position the head on the top of the staff and gently push the block about 1 inch (2.5 cm) onto the staff (figure 1).

3. Remove the foam block. Set the block down on a table with the traced shape facing up. With a sawing motion, use the table knife to cut away the foam around the shape you traced. Use the knife to round the sharp edges and to narrow the snout end.

4. Use the knife to cut the polystyrene foam egg in half lengthwise, and cut one half in half lengthwise again. These skinny slices will form the ears. Insert a toothpick in the rounded end of each ear. Put the ears in position on the head. (You may

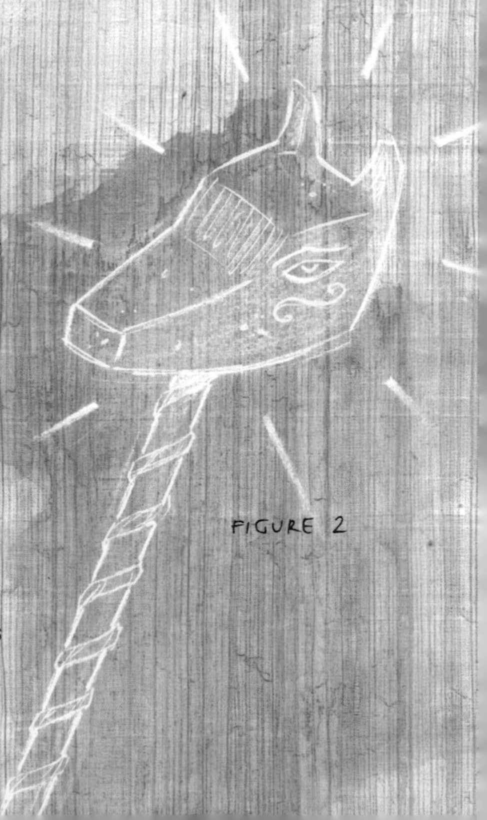

FIGURE 2

ENLARGE THIS TEMPLATE OF
THE HEAD OF ANUBIS TO MAKE
YOUR OWN STAFF.

Pyramid POWER

You just can't have an Egyptian party without pyramids! The architects of the great pyramids built the four walls out of massive stone blocks. Each wall faced a point of the compass—north, south, east, and west—and wall openings lined up with important stars in the sky. How big were they? Imagine walking three football fields laid end to end. That's the length of just one side of a pyramid at Giza, Egypt.

wish to trim the sharp edges further.) Secure the toothpicks in the ears with hot glue, and hot glue the ears to the head.

5. Tear the newspaper or tissue paper into 1/2-inch (1.3 cm) strips. If you want evenly torn strips, tear the paper by pulling up a strip against a ruler held down on the paper. You'll need a couple of good handfuls of strips. Set the strips aside.

6. In the small bowl, make a mixture of three parts of the white glue to one part water. Stir well.

7. Cover your working area with plastic sheeting or newspaper. Dip one strip of paper at a time into the bowl. Run the paper between your thumb and forefinger to wring out excess liquid.

8. Apply the strips to the head form, overlapping the edges and smoothing the strips as you work. Cover the form with one layer of strips, then

set the head aside to dry. Cover the bowl with the plastic wrap to keep the glue mixture from drying out.

9. Put at least three layers of paper strips on the form to make it smooth and strong. Allow each layer to dry overnight before adding the next layer.

10. When the final layer is dry, brush a coat of the gesso or acrylic primer on the head. Let it dry.

11. Paint the head gold or another color that matches your staff. Allow it to dry. Use the pencil to draw two Eyes of Horus on the head. Use a dark color to paint the eyes. Let dry.

12. Use a generous amount of hot glue to attach the head to the top of the staff (figure 2).

Sugar Cube Pyramids

Build sweet little pyramids made of sugar cubes (they're much easier to move than those huge granite blocks) for table decorations or a party activity. A pyramid building race might be fun.

WHAT YOU NEED
- 5-1/4 cups (630 g) confectioners' sugar
- mixing bowl
- sifter
- 1/2 cup (120 ml) egg whites
- 1 tablespoon and 1 1/2 teaspoons cream of tartar
- hand mixer
- damp towel
- waxed paper
- sugar cubes
- small, disposable knives
- white craft glue or hot glue (optional)

INSTRUCTIONS

1. To make edible "mortar" icing, sift the sugar after measuring it into a mixing bowl. Add the egg whites and cream of tartar. Use the hand mixer on low speed to mix the ingredients, then beat on high for two to five minutes until the icing is snow white and fluffy. Use the damp towel to cover the icing until you're ready to use it.

2. Build a solid base of sugar cubes five cubes square on the waxed paper. Use the knife to spread a tiny amount of icing on the sides of each cube to "glue" it to the next (use the glue for nonedible pyramids).

3. Spread a thin layer of icing on the first layer. Don't spread the icing to the edge. Build a second layer four cubes square. Spread a layer of icing on the second layer.

4. Build a third layer three cubes square, and a fourth layer two cubes square in the same way. Top the pyramid with a single cube.

5. Let the pyramid dry before moving it.

Paper Pyramids

Make paper pyramids to hold party favors or a Pyramid Pinata filled with goodies.

WHAT YOU NEED
- template (figure 1)
- scissors or craft knife
- construction paper, poster board, or corrugated board
- cellophane tape
- pencil
- colored pencils, crayons, or marking pens
- white craft glue or hot glue
- masking tape

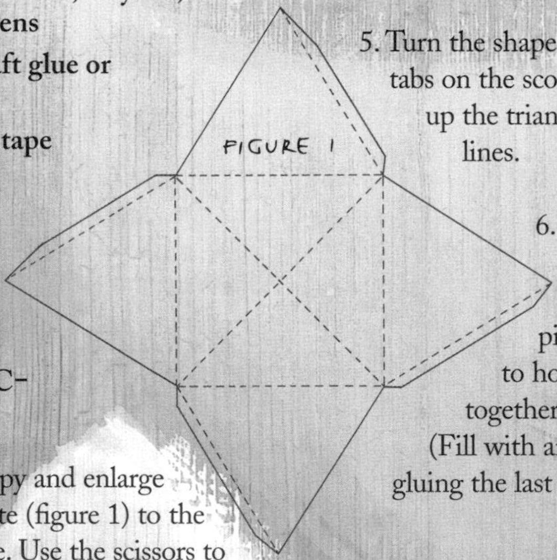

INSTRUCTIONS

1. Photocopy and enlarge the template (figure 1) to the desired size. Use the scissors to cut out the template along the solid lines.

2. Place the template on your chosen material, and use small strips of the tape to secure it. Use the pencil to trace around the outer edges and dotted lines of the template, pressing hard. You should be able to see the impressed lines on your material. Remove the template and cut out the shape.

3. Use the tip of the scissors or craft knife to score the impressed lines lightly.

4. Turn the shape over. Use colored pencils, crayons, or pens to suggest stonework on the shape (just a few horizontal lines on each triangle will be enough). For place cards, write the person's name on the pyramid. Use the hieroglyphic alphabet on page 95 for a real Egyptian touch!

5. Turn the shape over again. Fold the tabs on the scored lines. Then fold up the triangles on the scored lines.

6. Glue the tab of one triangle to the next, and use a small piece of masking tape to hold the triangles together until the glue dries. (Fill with any goodies before gluing the last triangle in place.)

FIGURE 1

Egyptian Fortune Catcher

Whether you think fortune-telling is silly or serious, folded paper "catchers" like this one have been used for many years by the young at heart, and this is a fun adaptation for your party. Guests can make them and take turns asking each other's catchers to answer their questions.

WHAT YOU NEED

- square piece of white paper, at least • 8 x 8 inches (20 x 20 cm)
- colored markers or pencils

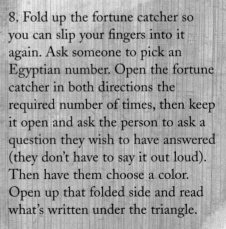

FIGURE 1

FIGURE 2

FIGURE 3

INSTRUCTIONS

1. Fold the paper in half—corner to corner—and open it up again. Then fold the paper in half using the other corners. Unfold the paper and you'll see an X-shape (figure 1).

2. Fold each corner to the center forming a smaller square (figure 2).

3. Turn the square over. Fold each corner to the center forming an even smaller square. Use the markers to color each of the eight small triangles a different color (figure 3).

4. Fold the square in half, top to bottom, then flatten it out. Fold the square in half again, side to side, and flatten it out.

5. Slip the index finger and thumb of each hand into the pockets that your folding created. Bring the points of the paper together. Now you can make the four pockets move (figure 4).

6. Lay the fortune catcher on the table with the pockets facing up. Number each square with the Egyptian numerals for 1, 3, 5, and 10.

7. Now open up the colored triangles and write short fortunes with Egyptian sayings like these under each: *"Anubis barks. No." "The Sphinx yawns. Maybe." "Pharaoh nods. Yes."* You get the idea.

8. Fold up the fortune catcher so you can slip your fingers into it again. Ask someone to pick an Egyptian number. Open the fortune catcher in both directions the required number of times, then keep it open and ask the person to ask a question they wish to have answered (they don't have to say it out loud). Then have them choose a color. Open up that folded side and read what's written under the triangle.

ONE

THREE

FIVE

TEN

Gaming

Secret Messages & other Sun Power Games

Alchemists and wizards often call upon the powers of the sun in their quest for the sorcerer's stone. Early scientists created heat and fire with sun rays too. A few hundred years ago, I knew a Frenchman named Lavoisier (lahv-WAH-see-ay) who even used solar power to melt iron. These party games should ALWAYS be played with an adult wizard present. Don't even THINK about starting them without a grown-up around, or I'll change you into a scarab beetle and you'll push dung balls around for the rest of your life.

Secret Message Game

WHAT YOU NEED

- a few sheets of white paper
- cup of warm tea
- small paintbrush
- candle and match (optional)
- small prizes (one prize per guest for the Secret Message Game, and only one for the Sun Ray Race)
- adult wizard
- magnifying glass (one large or a small one for each guest)
- disposable metal pie tins
- bright sunny day

INSTRUCTIONS

1. To make secret messages, prepare the paper first. Fold a sheet of the copy paper into four equal parts. Crease each fold well, then tear the paper into four pieces along the creased lines. Brew a cup of warm tea. Use the paintbrush and warm tea to stain the papers. Let them dry. If you wish, light the candle and singe the edges of the messages (do this only with an adult wizard present!).

2. Write a different "secret" message on each paper. For example, you could direct each guest to a spot (in a cabinet, behind a chair, under a garden bench, behind a bush) where a prize is hidden. Be sure to hide prizes there!

3. Assemble the players outdoors. The adult wizard should now show the players how to focus the sun's rays with the magnifying glass before starting the game. Explain that this is a way to harness the sun's energy and it must be used wisely!

4. Now give each player a secret message. Explain that it contains important clues to hidden treasure and mustn't fall into the wrong hands! Hand out the messages one at a time (or all at once if you have enough magnifying glasses). Direct the players to read their messages and memorize them.

5. The players should place their messages in the pie tins and use the magnifying glass to focus the sun's rays and burn up the message.

6. Once the message is burned, they can find their treasure. But not before!

Sun Ray Race

1. Give each player a secret message, magnifying glass, and pie tin.

2. Explain how to focus the ray's of the sun with a magnifying glass.

3. Give the start signal. The winner is the first person to set a secret message aflame. Give him or her a prize. If you wish, award smaller prizes for all players who manage to set their messages on fire.

Egyptian Dice and Dice Games

Egyptian legend says that dice were a gift from Thoth, the god of wisdom and numbers. Wood, ivory, and stone dice were found in ancient tombs, and the first dice were made from the ankle bones of sheep! A bit creepy, but that's where the phrase "throwing bones" comes from (it means playing with dice). Egyptian wizards used dice to tell the future. They also liked to play mind games to see who could roll the dice the best—without touching them!

Making the Dice

WHAT YOU NEED

- die template
- thin card stock
- scissors
- glue sticks
- rubber bands
- dried small beans, peas, or rice

TEMPLATE TO MAKE
THE DICE, ENLARGE 150%

INSTRUCTIONS

1. Go to a copy store and have the template on this page photocopied onto thin card stock. You'll need two copies for each pair of dice.

2. Use the scissors to cut out the copies.

3. Use the tip of the scissors to lightly score the dotted lines. Be careful, don't cut through the paper.

4. Fold the tabs away from the printed side of the pattern.

5. Spread glue on the tabs at points A. Glue the tabs to the inside of the first two squares. Use your fingers to press the tabs to the squares.

6. Spread glue on the next tabs. Glue them to the square and press the tabs firmly with your fingers.

7. Place a small spoonful of dried peas in the die before you glue the last side.

8. Glue the last side. Stretch a rubber band around the die to hold it in place until the glue dries.

9. Repeat for the other die.

Dice Game #1
(for four to six players)

When you explain this game to your guests, play a couple of teaching rounds so everyone understands how it works. This game is easy to learn and requires little adult supervision.

WHAT YOU NEED

- 1 die
- 6 cups
- peanuts, jelly beans, sunflower seeds, or any small snack food

HOW TO PLAY

The first player rolls the die and has to put one peanut or other snack in the corresponding cup. For example, if the first player rolls a 5, he has to put a peanut or other snack in cup 5. The second player now rolls. If she rolls a 5, she can eat or keep the contents of cup 5. Otherwise, the second player must put something in the cup which corresponds to the number she rolled.

In other words, if a player rolls the die and the cup that matches the number is empty, the player must place something in the cup. If a cup has something in it, the player keeps the treat. Either way, the player must continue to roll the die until he has to place something in an empty cup. For example, cups 2 and 5 have something in them. The player rolls a 2. They get what is in cup 2. It is still the player's turn until he rolls a 1, 2, or 6. (You can eat a lot of snacks this way!)

Dice Game #2
(for an unlimited number of players)

This game is slightly more complicated and requires a bit more adult supervision.

WHAT YOU NEED

- 1 pair of dice
- snacks or small prizes
- paper and pencil (optional)

HOW TO PLAY

Have each player roll the dice and remember the number they rolled (or write it down). The person with the highest roll starts first. Next, player number one rolls the dice. If a 7 or 11 is rolled, the player automatically wins a prize and rolls again. However, if player number one throws a 2, 3, or 12, he loses his turn and must pass the dice to the player who rolled the second highest number (when everyone rolled the dice the first time).

However, if the first player rolls a 4, 5, 6, 8, 9, or 10, that number becomes the player's point and she continues to roll. If she throws the same point again, she wins a prize! But if the player rolls a 7, she loses the right to throw again and must pass the dice to the next player.

The Yes/No Pendulum Game

We all want answers to questions about the future, such as "Am I going to grow up to be a really great wizard?" A pendulum (PEN-due-lumm) is a weight on a string that swings back and forth as it feels energy from people and objects. Party guests can use this board game to ask questions that can be answered with a yes or no. Add the Egyptian Dice (page 101) for more fun.

WHAT YOU NEED

• poster board, 10 inches (25.4 cm)
• square
• ruler
• fine-tip permanent marker
• hieroglyphic alphabet on page 95 (optional)
• bead cap, in a diameter that matches the diameter of the quartz*
• quick-dry glue
• small, pointed piece of quartz or other mineral
• jewelry chain or string, 9 inches (22.9 cm) long
• 1 die from the Egyptian Dice (optional)

*Available at bead stores

INSTRUCTIONS

1. To make the answer board, use the ruler to measure to the centerpoint of the poster board and mark it with the marker. Use the marker to draw two 8-inch (20.3 cm) lines, forming a cross in the middle of the board.

2. Write the word "Yes" at both ends of one line, and "No" at both ends of the other line. If you wish, write them in hieroglyphs by copying the symbols on page 95.

3. To make the pendulum, apply a little quick-dry glue inside the bead cap, and attach it to the bluntest end of the piece of quartz, bending the cap to fit. Let dry.

4. Thread one end of the chain or string through the loop on the fastener. Tie it in place. Apply a dot of glue to the knot. Let dry.

5. Put the answer board on a tabletop and have the players sit quietly around it. One at a time, each player should hold the chain about 7 inches (17.8 cm) from the pendulum so the pendulum hangs about 1/2 inch (1.3 cm) above the center of the cross but doesn't touch the board.

6. Keeping his mind focused and hand still, the player can now ask any question that can be answered "yes" or "no."

7. The pendulum will start to swing by itself along the "yes" or "no" line of the answer board. If it moves in a circle or stays still, try asking the question a different way.

8. Players can combine what the pendulum says with throws of one die. Think of a question, and roll the die. Tradition says that certain numbers predict certain things. One is a good sign. Two is a bad sign. Three, be careful. Four, review your potential choices for action. Five, be patient, things will gradually improve. Six, proceed with your plans!

Feasting

Sand Patties

These potato patties are so good, even the fussiest camel will eat one and not spit it back at you. I think some Irish wizards introduced them to Egyptian sorcerers at a magicians' conference a long time ago, and that's how the potato made it to Egypt.

ADULT WIZARD SUPERVISION!

WHAT YOU NEED

Yield: 24 1½-inch (3.8 cm) patties

- adult wizard
- 6 to 8 large potatoes
- kitchen knife
- large saucepan
- water
- 1 tablespoon (15 mL) vegetable oil
- 2 pinches black or yellow mustard seeds
- 3 cloves garlic
- 1 small onion
- ½ cup (100 g) fresh cilantro (optional)
- 2 tablespoons (30 mL) lemon juice
- 2 pinches salt
- skillet

INSTRUCTIONS

1. Get an adult wizard to peel the potatoes and slice them into small cubes. Put the cubes in the saucepan and cover them with water.

2. Bring the water to a boil. Reduce the heat and simmer about 20 minutes, until the potatoes are tender.

3. Drain off the water and mash the potatoes.

4. Heat the vegetable oil in a skillet over medium high heat. Add the mustard seeds and fry them until they pop.

5. Slice the garlic into thin sections and fry it with the mustard seeds for about 20 seconds.

6. Stir the garlic and the mustard seeds into the potatoes. Chop the onion into small pieces and add them to the potatoes. Stir in the cilantro, lemon juice, and salt.

7. Shape the potatoes into patties, about 1½ inches (3.8 cm) wide. Fry them in batches in a lightly oiled skillet over medium-high heat until they're brown on both sides. This should take one to two minutes per side.

8. Cool slightly and serve.

SUN TEA, ANYONE?

Ra Herbal Sun Tea

Does the power of mighty Ra, the Egyptian sun god, flow into this tea as it brews? Whether you believe it or not, it tastes good anyway.

WHAT YOU NEED

- large glass jar with lid
- herbal tea bags
- water
- a sunny day
- sugar or honey (optional)

INSTRUCTIONS

1. Fill the jar with water. Add the tea bags and cover with the lid.

2. Put the jar in a sunny window and let it sit for at least 30 minutes. The tea may take longer to steep if it's a cool day. You'll know it's ready when the the herbs change the color of the water.

3. Add the sugar or honey to taste, and serve chilled.

The Pharaoh's Final Rest,

AS TOLD BY THE WIZARD

On the banks of the Nile, 4,500 years ago, Pharaoh Khufu (FAIR-oh KOO-FOO) summoned his chief wizard. (No, not me, even *I'm* not that old.) Khufu wanted to build a tomb for himself that would never be equalled. The wizard gave good advice, and Khufu built the Great Pyramid at Giza, one of the Seven Wonders of the World.

When Khufu died, his mummy was buried in the Great Pyramid with everything the king needed for the afterlife. The tomb held gold and gems, a metal that would never rust, and a piece of glass that could be bent in half without shattering. More than 1,000 years later, stories of the tomb reached the ears of Al-Mamun (AL-ma-moon), the ruler of Baghdad (BAG-dad). Al-Mamun broke into the tomb but found only Khufu's empty coffin. Someone had already stolen every-thing! I don't know what happened to that unknown grave robber, but I have a feeling it was very, very bad.

Legends say the royal tombs were full of deadly snakes and blood-sucking bats the size of men. Robbers came anyway. But did the Pharaohs have their own way of dealing with the thieves? Let me tell you about King Tut's tomb and the curse of the pharaohs.

In the 1800s, an English archaeol-ogist (AR-kee-ALL-uh-jist) named Howard Carver studied ancient Egypt for a long time. Carver believed that, just maybe, the tomb of a pharaoh named Tutankhamun (TOOT-ung-KAH-muhn, or Tut for short) had escaped the attention of grave robbers. Tut became king when he was nine years old, and he died at age 18. Carver searched Egypt's Valley of Kings for years, looking for the tomb. Carver had a rich patron, the English Lord Carnarvon, who paid for the search.

A servant gave Carver a yellow canary to bring luck to the expedition. One week later, Carver found Tut's tomb! Returning home late that night, tired but excited, the explorer was met by his servant. That very day, when the tomb was discovered, a cobra had slithered into the house and killed the canary. The servant knew that cobras were the ancient symbols of the Pharaoh's power. He begged Carver not to open the tomb. But Carver ignored him and opened the tomb the next day.

Legend says that one of the first things they found in the tomb was a small clay tablet. It read, "Death shall slay with its wings/Whoever disturbs the peace of kings." Carver and the English lord also found piles of gold and jewels, and they ignored the warning on the tablet. A few months after their discovery, the two men had a terrible fight. Lord Carnarvon want-ed to take half the treasure back to his estate in Britain. Carver thought it should all stay in Egypt, in the muse-um at Cairo. They fought bitterly and parted ways.

One month later and without warning, Lord Carnarvon became very ill. He died in Cairo one week later. At the moment of his death, every light in the city went out, and his favorite dog, thousands of miles away, howled once and fell over dead. For years after that, anyone who came in contact with objects from Tut's tomb died suddenly or had terrible accidents. Finally, Tut's treasures were returned to the museum of Cairo, and the strange events stopped. The Pharaoh's body remains in his tomb at Giza, and I for one sincerely hope he is resting peacefully.

Spirited DRUID HALLOWEEN Gathering

The Druids were the most important wizards in Great Britain long ago. They must have really liked parties, because their ghosts still dance and sing! Welsh people say you can still hear voices and the sounds of pattering feet near ancient stones. Here are my secrets for giving a Halloween party to please all your Druid friends and friendly spirits.

Party Decorations

Halloween is the best night of the year for all things wizardly. That's because the line between the human and spirit worlds grows very, very thin. The Celtic (KELL-tick) people of long ago—and their Druid (DREW-id) wizards—knew this, of course. They made special magic and burned bonfires to invite good spirits to visit and to keep away the bad ones. Fairies are very active this night too.

Decorate your party room to make ghostly guests feel welcome. In Scotland and Wales, people used to set out "dumb suppers" of oatmeal and milk for visiting ghosts. Why not set out a plate of party food for your own ghosts? Spirits like blue lights, so screw blue party bulbs into lamps and ceiling fixtures, or burn candles in blue glass votive holders. To keep away any mean fairies, decorate the room with horseshoes. (Paper horseshoe cutouts work too. Just the shape makes them think twice.)

In case you don't yet have the power to see ghosts, you can make your own. Buy some purple or black balloons, glow-in-the-dark paint, and an ultraviolet light (called a "black" light) at the hardware store. Blow up the balloons, and paint ghost faces on them. Tape them to the ceiling. Turn off the regular lights, turn on the black light, and your ghosts will appear! Ghosts like to travel with bats, too, so trace the bat on this page onto black construction paper or poster board. Glue a piece of fishing line between two bat cutouts, making a "sandwich." Tape the bats to the ceilings, window frames, and doorways.

Druids made their best magic in groves of oak trees, and lots of fairies live in the trees' big branches. So bring a Halloween forest inside your party! Trace the oak leaf pattern on page 85 and make as many cutouts as you like from gold, silver, or colored construction paper. Add leaf "veins" of puff paint and glitter. Use a large needle and upholstery thread to string the leaves together, then hang them up. It's fun to completely cover furniture, lamp shades, or even a big pumpkin with leaves too. Don't have time to make cutouts? Gather dried leaves from your backyard, put them on newspaper, and spray them with gold or silver paint. Let dry, then string them up and scatter them around.

Halloween is also the best time to see into the future. Set up tables for party guests to read palms or tea leaves and to play the Yes/No Pendulum Game (pages 129 and 103). Hand out bells and ask guests to make as much noise as they can for a little while. (Bad ghosts hate the sound of bells.)

Goddesses and wizards make their best potions in pots called cauldrons, and your friends can have fun making their own take-home cauldrons (page 13). The Druids thought people's heads carried big magic, so why not decorate your table with "heads" of cabbage, plus good-luck nuts and apples? You can use them later for Cabbage Bowling, Magic Nuts Tic Tac Toe, and Druid Apple Ducking (pages 114 and 115).

ALL IN THE SPIRIT OF GOOD FUN!

Druid Robe

Most Druids lived in northern countries and had to dress warmly. Their wool robes were dyed with roots and berries, and wild animals' thick pelts made fine winter cloaks. Belt your robe with a Magic Girdle, and stick a Dagger in it (pages 56 and 111).

WHAT YOU NEED

- Basic Robe on page 135, made with a solid, dark-color fabric
- 1 1/2 yards of fake fur (optional)

INSTRUCTIONS

1. Follow the directions for the Basic Robe. As a rule, Druids dressed in simple, dark robes decorated only by the gleam of metal or sheen of fur.

2. Cut the fake fur yardage so that it has an animal shape (head, four legs) rather than a simple rectangle.

3. Drape the fur over your shoulder and gird your waist with the Magic Girdle. Add a dagger and Celtic jewelry (page 111) if desired.

Goddess of Beauty Tunic, Crown, & Magic Girdle

Cliodna (KLEE-nah) is the legendary Celtic goddess of beauty, magic, love, and healing. She wears a short tunic gathered with a girdle of silver spirals. Her crown is adorned with ocean waves, seashells, and a silvery moon, because the sea is so important to her story. The beautiful daughter of the last Druid in Ireland, Cliodna fell in love with a handsome human and ran away with him. Hungry and tired, they reached the island's rocky shore, where a jealous sea god lulled them into a deep, magical sleep. He sent a large wave to drown Cliodna's sweetheart and to sweep her to the Land of Promise. She rules there today and sometimes changes shape into a soaring seabird or a large wave.

WHAT YOU NEED
(for the tunic)

- **Basic Robe on page 135, made with thin cotton fabric***
- **silver acrylic paint and fabric medium (optional)**

*Modify the instructions as explained below.

INSTRUCTIONS

1. In step 1 of the basic instructions, measure the width of the shoulders rather than measuring from wrist to wrist. Add 6 inches (15.2 cm) to the width of the shoulders. For a shorter tunic, measure only from the knee to the shoulder instead of from the shoulder to the floor.

2. In step 2, divide the shoulder width measurement by 2. Measure and mark this measurement from the folded edge.

3. Skip step 5.

4. In step 6, draw the line from the open edge at the bottom of the fabric to the mark you made in step 2 for the shoulder width.

5. Cut the fabric as directed. Open up the robe.

6. Sew the side seams starting at the hem to approximately 12 inches (30.5 cm) from the folded shoulder line.

7. Paint a band of silver crescent moons or waves around the hem if desired, following the decorating directions on page 137.

WHAT YOU NEED
(for the crown)

- **Fillet materials on page 55**
- **mallet or small hammer**
- **small seashells or jewels (optional)**
- **scrap piece of oven liner (optional)**
- **scouring pad (optional)**

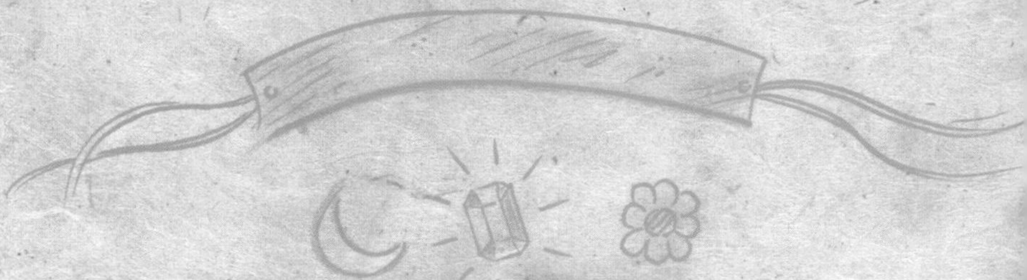

INSTRUCTIONS

1. Follow steps 1 through 4 of the instructions on page 55 to make a fillet. Bend the wire into a wavy pattern (figure 1). Hammer the fillet and finish it as directed (figure 2).

2. If desired, hot glue the seashells to the crown. Cut a crescent moon shape from the oven liner. Use the scouring pad on the edges to remove any sharpness, and hot glue the moon to the crown.

FIGURE 1

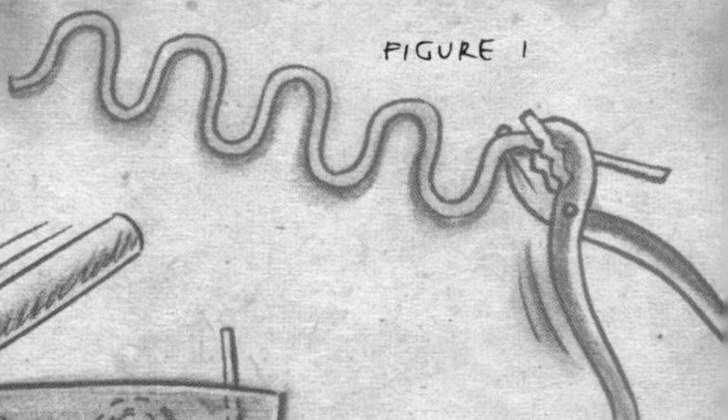

FIGURE 2

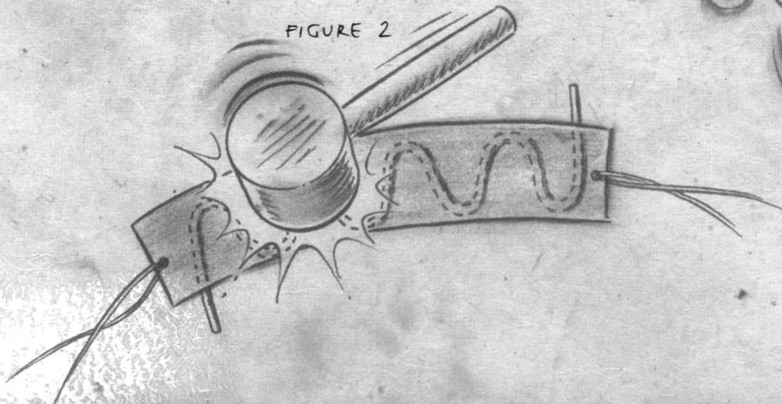

Celtic Jewelry

The Celts made such beautiful metalwork, some people thought wizards taught them how do it. They made sharp daggers, headgear, and jewelry, and wore wrist cuffs for beauty and for wrist protection in sword fights. Their heavy neck collars called torques (TORKS) were highly prized as war booty by other tribes. You won't need a blacksmith's tools to make yours, though. A quick trip to the grocery and hardware store will provide the materials you need.

WHAT YOU NEED (for the girdle)

- long piece of string
- scissors
- torque materials on page 112

INSTRUCTIONS

1. Wrap a string around your waist to determine how long your girdle will be. Measure the string, and add 18 to 24 inches (45.7 to 61 cm) to the measurement to allow for a tie. Measure and cut two lengths of string to this measurement (figure 1).

2. Follow the directions on page 112 for making silver spirals. Make enough to almost fill the piece of string you cut.

3. Thread the spirals as directed in steps 11 through 13 of the directions on page 113.

WHAT YOU NEED (for the Wrist Cuff)

- cuff template on page 112
- scissors
- oven liner
- cellophane tape
- metal soup spoon
- kitchen abrasive pad
- magazine or newspaper
- ball-point pen
- wooden chopstick or handle of small paintbrush
- colored markers (optional)
- plastic or glass jewels, stones, or shells
- hot-glue gun and glue stick
- hole punch
- silver tinsel stem

INSTRUCTIONS

1. Photocopy the cuff template on page 112 and use the scissors to cut it out.

2. Tape the cutout to the oven liner. Cut around the template. Don't throw the template away!

3. Lay the cuff on a smooth surface. Use the soup spoon to rub the surface of the metal to remove any pattern, then turn it over and rub the other side.

4. Use the abrasive pad to scour the cuff and give it a matte surface.

5. Tape the template to the flattened cuff.

6. Lay the cuff on the magazine, template side up. Working on the center of the cuff first, use the ball-point pen to trace the central spiral outline. Press hard! Trace the curved shapes inside the outline to fill it in. Trace the outer circle in the same way.

III

WHAT YOU NEED
(for the Torque)

- lead-free, solid wire solder (.125 diameter)*
  - ruler
  - wire cutters or old scissors
  - fine-tip permanent marker
  - needle-nose pliers
- household pliers
- thin-gauge wire, 24-gauge or thinner (optional)
- thin cord (optional)

*Available in plumbing supply stores. Wire solder looks like a heavy gauge silver wire but is much easier to shape than real wire. The equivalent British Standard or Imperial wire gauge is 0.022.

INSTRUCTIONS

1. Use the wire cutters or scissors to cut 15-inch (38 cm) lengths of the wire solder. You'll need a length for each double spiral. Set aside.

2. Mark the center of a length of wire with the permanent marker.

3. Use the needle-nose pliers to make a tight circular loop at each end of the wire (figure 1). Hold the loop flat with the household pliers and begin coiling the wire around the loop. (The solder wire is soft enough to coil easily.) After a few turns, you can continue to tightly coil, holding the initial loop between your thumb and forefinger. Coil to the center mark, then coil the other end in the same way (figure 2).

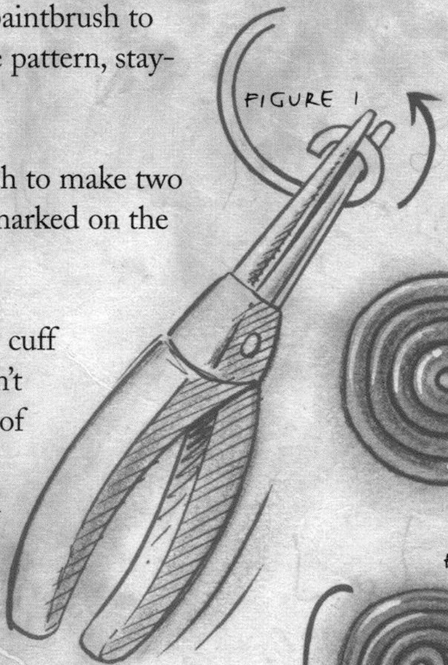

4. Hold the coils with both hands and twist the coils in opposite directions (figure 3). Roll both coils until they meet.

5. Repeat steps 2 through 4 for each double spiral you wish to make.

6. You can make your torque with several spirals or only one. If you want to make a single-spiral torque, measure and cut 18 inches (46 cm) of wire solder. Fold the long piece of wire into a long U shape. Thread the ends through the centers of the double spiral you made in steps 3 and 4.

7. Pressing hard, trace the spiral edge patterns.

8. Turn over the cuff. To raise the circular pattern, use the small, blunt end of the chopstick or paintbrush to lightly rub inside the pattern, staying inside the lines.

9. Use the hole punch to make two holes in the cuff as marked on the pattern.

10. Gently curve the cuff to fit your wrist. Don't press too hard or all of your hard work embossing the metal will disappear!

11. Thread the tinsel stem through the holes. Twist together the ends of the stem to secure the cuff on your wrist.

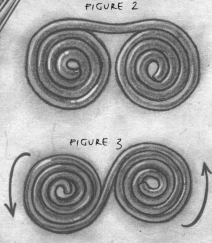

FIGURE 1

FIGURE 2

FIGURE 3

7. Using the needle-nose pliers, make an open loop at each end of the wire.

8. Gently shape the long wire into a circle. Twist one of the loops to interlock with the other loop. This will make the "catch" for the torque.

9. To make a multispiral torque, lay the spirals in a line on a flat surface.

10. Measure and cut two 36-inch (91 cm) lengths of the thin-gauge wire or twine.

11. Thread one length of the twine or wire down through the center of a spiral and back up through the next center. Continue to thread all of the spirals in this way.

12. Thread the second length of twine or wire from the back, up through the front center, and down through the next center. Thread the rest of the spirals the same way.

13. At the end of the line of spirals, secure them by knotting the lengths of twine or twisting the wires together near the last spiral.

14. Knot or twist the ends together, and slip the torque over your head.

Turnip Toss

You'll need to play this game outside in daylight, but long ago the Irish made turnips into tiny lanterns, hollowing them out and carving little faces on them. On Halloween night, they carried them to keep bad ghosts away. The Scots also sang a song about it:

Halloween night of fire
A candle in a cabbage stem
A turnip lantern with glowing eyes
To scare both witch and warlock

WHAT YOU NEED

• turnip
• paved drive, patio, or grassy lawn, with a wall or structure tall enough to keep the teams from seeing each other
• adult referee

INSTRUCTIONS

1. Separate the players into two teams, one on each side of the wall or structure so they're hidden from each other.

2. To start the game, one player throws the turnip over the top, as high as he likes and in the direction he chooses.

3. If the other team fail to catch the turnip, someone should pick it up and throw it back over.

4. If a player catches the turnip on its way down, he should run around the corner, using the turnip to touch-tag as many people on the other team as possible in 30 seconds. The other team, meanwhile, are all running away!

5. After 30 seconds, the referee calls time. The original catcher and anyone who was "tagged" go back to the other side of the wall.

6. The game is over when all the players have been tagged and everyone's on the same side of the wall!

Cabbage Bowling

This bowling game uses a vegetable that was very popular in Scotland at Halloween. People made jack-o'-lanterns from the hollowed-out stems of cabbage plants. If a Scotsman had to go out on Halloween night, he carried one with a lit candle inside to frighten away evil spirits. (Between you and me, I think it was the smell of burning cabbage that scared them off!)

WHAT YOU NEED

- 10 clean, empty 2-liter plastic soda bottles with screw-on tops
- sand or water
- rope or chalk
- large head of cabbage (plus some extras in case of accidental cabbage explosion)
- notepad or piece of paper
- pencil

INSTRUCTIONS

1. Weight the soda bottles by filling them with a little sand or water, and screw the tops on tightly.

2. Decide where the starting line will be, and set the bottles up about 20 feet away. Arrange them in a circle 8 feet (2.4 m) across, with the bottles spaced far enough apart so the cabbage can pass between them.

3. Use the rope or chalk to mark the starting line.

4. Players should stand behind the starting line. The goal is to knock down the bottles by rolling the cabbage like a bowling ball. Each player gets three tries per turn, with a point won for each bottle knocked down. But there's a trick! The five bottles in the back of the circle count for two points each, and if you hit one of the front bottles while aiming for a back bottle, you lose a point.

5. After a player finishes her three tries, note her points in the notepad and set up the bottles for the next player.

6. Keep playing until someone wins 21 points or more.

Druid Apple Ducking

Did you know the Druids sometimes used cauldrons or pools of water to help them see into the future? You'll play blindfolded, and use your mental powers to "see" the apple you want.

WHAT YOU NEED

- large washtub of water
- piece of plastic or shower curtain
- apples in red, yellow, and green colors, one per player
- blindfold
- magic wand or long-handled spoon
- adult wizard
- towel
- prizes, one per player
- shovel (optional)

INSTRUCTIONS

1. Prepare the prizes, matching one type of prize per apple color. Everyone who catches a green apple, for example, might win a Basilisk Protection Device (page 44), while the red apples win a sack of Alchemist's Gold (page 19).

2. Lay the shower curtain on the floor. Put the tub on top and fill with water. Dump in the apples.

3. While an adult wizard uses the wand or spoon to stir the water to keep the apples constantly moving, a blindfolded player kneels by the tub.

4. Now it's up to the player to use her mental powers to catch the color apple she wants with her teeth! Award prizes. Keep the towel handy for splashes.

5. Now eat the apples, or use the shovel to bury them outside as unicorn bait.

Magic Nuts Tic Tac Toe

The hazel tree was the Druid tree of knowledge, and Italian wizards used walnut trees to help see into the future. (Almonds are my own favorite snack.)

WHAT YOU NEED

- white poster board, 24 x 36 inches*
- ruler
- pencil
- craft knife or scissors
- oak leaf pattern
- acrylic paints, including gold
- paintbrush
- gel pens in colors of your choice
- mixture of hazelnuts, walnuts, and almonds still in their shells, 18 nuts per game board
- nutcrackers

*One piece of poster board makes six game cards.

INSTRUCTIONS

1. Measure and mark the poster board to make six square game cards, each 12 inches (30.5 cm) square. Cut them out.

2. Photocopy the oak leaf pattern and carefully cut out the leaf shape. Paint the nuts gold and let dry.

3. Trace the leaf onto the game cards. Paint as desired and let dry. Use the ruler and gel pens to draw four lines on each card (figure 1).

4. Two people can play this game. Give each team one card and 18 nuts.

5. When the adult wizard gives the signal, the first team that uses the same nut to cover a row on the card should jump up and yell something magical such as, "*Hocus pocus hazelnuts!*" or "*Wizardly walnuts!*" When the game is over, shell the nuts and eat!

FIGURE 1

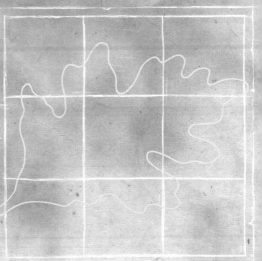

Feasting

Ghost Pizza

ADULT WIZARD SUPERVISION!

Since ghosts are see-through, have you ever wondered what happens when they eat? I firmly believe there are some things you just don't want to see! Ask any ghostly party guests to wear white sheets when they dine to be polite to the other guests.

WHAT YOU NEED

• 2 prepared 12-inch (30.5 cm) pizza crusts
• olive oil
• baking sheet
• 6 ounces (90 g) mozzarella, feta cheese, or both
• 2 tablespoons (30 mL) chopped garlic (optional)
• 1 teaspoon dried rosemary

INSTRUCTIONS

1. Brush the pizza crusts generously with the olive oil.

2. Sprinkle the crusts with the cheese. Saute the garlic in a little of the olive oil until soft, then sprinkle over the pizzas. Sprinkle with the rosemary and drizzle a little more oil on top of the pizzas.

3. Put the pizzas on the baking sheet and bake them on the bottom rack of the oven according to the directions for the pizza crust.

4. After baking, remove the pizzas from the oven and let cool for five minutes before serving.

Handwiches

It can be difficult having goblins over for dinner. They'll eat everything in sight! Where did you think the phrase, "gobbling your food" came from, anyway? I always make sure I have stacks of these sandwiches around for goblin guests, so they won't bite the hand that feeds them.

WHAT YOU NEED

• piece of cardboard
• pencil
• craft knife
• large loaf of sliced bread
• sharp bread knife or scissors
• sandwich filling, such as cream cheese

INSTRUCTIONS

1. Spread slices of bread with the sandwich filling. Top with another slice of bread.

2. Place someone's hand (still attached to the rest of them) atop the cardboard. The hand should be small enough to fit on a slice of bread. Use the pencil to trace the hand, then cut it out with the craft knife.

3. Place the cardboard template atop each sandwich and use the bread knife or scissors to cut away the excess, creating a hand shape.

Jellied Sugar Snails

A little-known legend tells the tale of the Great Snail Invasion of the British Isles, when the islands started to sink beneath the weight of millions of the slimy creatures. Lugh Lamfota the Long Arm, one of Scotland's biggest, blondest heroes, saved the day by scooping up the snail chieftains and throwing them in the ocean, which was miles away. The other snails fled (as fast as a snail can flee, mind you) and to this day, people eat Jellied Sugar Snails to celebrate the victory.

WHAT YOU NEED

Yield: about 50 snails

- butter
- baking pan, 8 x 8 inches (20.5 x 20.5 cm)
- $1/2$ cup (120 mL) water
- 2 cups (400 g) granulated sugar
- medium saucepan
- candy thermometer
- $2^1/2$ tablespoons (37.5 g) gelatin
- $1/4$ cup (60 mL) cold water
- small mixing bowl
- $3/4$ cup (180 mL) lime juice
- green food coloring
- whisk
- cutting board
- sharp knife
- $1/8$ cup (25 g) superfine sugar

INSTRUCTIONS

1. Butter the baking pan and set aside.

2. Combine the water and sugar in the medium saucepan, and clip the candy thermometer to the side of the pan. Cook over medium heat until the mixture reaches 255°F (123°C).

3. Soak the gelatin in the cold water in a small mixing bowl for about five minutes, then add it to cooked syrup. Remove from heat, add the lime juice and a few drops of the food coloring, and use the whisk to blend the mixture.

4. Pour the mixture into the buttered baking pan. Set aside for several hours, until firm.

5. Turn the pan out onto the cutting board. Use the knife to slice the gelled mixture into rectangular snail shapes and roll them in the superfine sugar.

Chocolate Covered Worms

Maybe it's best not to dwell on this, but ghouls and goblins love to snack on squirmy, wriggly things. Here's how to make some for guests with strong stomachs!

WHAT YOU NEED

- waxed paper
- small microwaveable bowl
- 12-oz. (330 g) bag of semisweet chocolate chips
- spoon
- gelatin candy in the shape of worms
- tongs

INSTRUCTIONS

1. Spread a sheet of the waxed paper on your work surface.

2. Put the chocolate chips in the small bowl. Microwave it on high power for 1 minute, then stir the chocolate thoroughly. Continue heating and stirring in 20-second intervals until the chocolate is melted. Be careful not to burn it!

3. Drop the gelatin worms into the chocolate. Use the tongs to remove them one at time and place them on the waxed paper. Let sit until the chocolate is firm.

THE Beheading Ball

This is the story of a king's yearly Halloween banquet. Halloween is the favorite holiday of magical folks, but sometimes people in his court got spooked by all the wizards, fairies, and ghosts who showed up. One year, the king gave in to the complaints and invited only regular people to his banquet. So there were no more ghosts to do invisibility tricks, no wizards to set off fireworks, and no three-headed beasts to meet. It didn't seem like Halloween at all!

One year, just as the pumpkin pie was being served, a giant tramped into the feasting hall, lugging a huge, bloody axe. He jumped on a table and shouted, "It's time to play the Beheading Game!" He swung the axe around wildly, nearly chopping a hole in the roof while everyone dove for cover. "One of you chops off my head with this axe, then I chop off yours," the Giant boomed.

The King's chief knight thought, "How can he chop off my head if I've already chopped off his? What a stupid giant!" He said, "I'll play." The giant handed over the axe and knelt on the floor. The knight raised the axe high, and struck the giant so hard his head spun across the room and smacked into a wall. The knight smirked, then he turned and bowed. The king couldn't finish his dessert, and his advisors frowned. This was no way to treat a guest, not even an uninvited one!

Then the headless body stirred. It reached for the axe, and the giant's head said, "My turn!" The knight turned white as a sheet, dropped the axe, and ran out of the hall. "Foul play!" bellowed the giant. He stood, picked up his head, tucked it under his arm, and walked out. Some people whispered, "This is why we don't invite them."

The giant wasn't seen again, but as Halloween drew near, the very thought gave the king a terrible headache. He even suggested changing the date of the banquet to fool the giant. But his advisors pursed their lips, shook their heads, and declared that this was a very bad idea. The Halloween banquet should be on Halloween. And so it was.

This time, the giant burst in halfway through the meal, his head again atop his body. He shouted, "It's time to play the Beheading Game! Just like last year, remember? One of you chops off my head with this axe, then I chop off yours. Who's in?" The hall fell silent. Finally a young squire who was new to the kingdom spoke up. "It's just a game, right?" he asked.

"Of course," said the giant.

"I don't know if I can pick up your axe," the squire said. "Could I use my sword instead?"

"NO!" the giant shouted, "We use my axe or we don't play at all!"

"Okay, okay," the squire agreed hastily. "What if you lie down on the floor? Then I won't have lift it so high."

The giant laid down. The squire grasped the axe with both hands. Straining with all his might, he picked it up—and chopped off the giant's head. It rolled under a table. The headless giant stood and said, "My turn." The squire swallowed twice, turned down his collar, laid his head on the table, and squeezed his eyes shut. The giant swung the axe, and the young squire's head plopped upon the floor. The squire stood up, confused. What was that he saw? The ceiling? Someone's legs? Suddenly he realized he wasn't dead, although his head lay on the floor. Then the giant laughed and laughed, and the squire's head chuckled too, its eyes crinkling with laughter.

Because of the squire's bravery, everyone realized that the giant's axe was magic—it didn't kill anyone! Everyone, including the giant and the squire, started trading heads for fun. At evening's end, they put their own heads back on and went home. And from that time forward, everyone was welcome at the Halloween banquet, now named the Beheading Ball.

THINGS THAT GO BUMP IN THE NIGHT:
How to Know if You're Being VISITED by GHOSTS
AND HOW TO ESCAPE IF YOU WANT TO

Some clues that you have ghostly visitors are just so obvious, you'd have to be a DUMBKOPF to miss them. That's what my German friend, Doctor Van Helsing, used to say. That prickly feeling on the back of your neck, the sudden chill that turns your skin to goosebumps. . . Of course, it all depends on whether ghosts bother you or not. Friendly ghosts can be very good company for wizards during a long night by the fire. There are other clues, some of them not as well known.

You know you've got visitors when...
• a candle flame burns blue or blows out suddenly.• you suddenly smell flowers or spices.• your dog or cat starts to look very hard at an empty corner of the room. • you see lights moving about and they vanish when you get closer.

If you're outside, don't follow one! It could be a will-o'-the-wisp trying to lure you into a swamp where you'll drown. • you see a little cloud of dust travelling along the ground. (If you want to rescue someone who's been kidnapped to Fairyland, throw a little road dust from your footprint on the cloud. The fairies will have to do what you ask.) • you hear the sound of a stick breaking while you're out walking at night. • a bat flies into the house.

How to See Ghosts
• Keep your eyes wide open on Halloween. It's the best night of the year to spot spirits. • Stand behind your dog and peer out from between its ears.
• Hold up a ring and look through it (this works with keyholes, too).
• Go wait by a crossroads (especially on Halloween).

How to Drive Away or Escape Ghosts
• Keep a light burning in a room at night. • Carve a jack-o'-lantern.
• Throw a house key at the spirit.• If you're close to a brook or stream, jump over. Ghosts can't cross water. • Sprinkle ashes on the floor. Once they walk through them, they won't return. (Ghosts like to keep clean, you know.) • Put a net over your window, door, or keyhole. A kitchen strainer works too. Ghosts have to count every hole before they can come in, and by then it's daylight.

The World's Shortest GHOST STORIES

Ever since I was a young wizard in knee pants, these two stories have always made me laugh and given me a little thrill at the same time. Try telling them at a spend-the-night party. Your guests may not sleep, but they probably weren't planning to anyway.

Short Story Number One #1
An overnight guest at a castle was given a haunted room to sleep in. Nervous, he locked the door, slammed the shutters closed, peeked under the bed, and made sure the closets were empty. Quickly, he got into bed. Just as he blew out the candle, a tiny voice spoke from the curtains at the head of the bed, "There now, we're all shut in for the night."

Even Shorter Story Number Two #2
He woke up all alone in the middle of the night, feeling frightened. As he reached for the matches in the dark, they were placed, gently, in his hand.

Wizard's WINTER Revels

Ages ago, during the dark days of winter, people had special celebrations to encourage the sun to come back. They lit fires and gave presents to forest spirits, so the trees would grow green again. Learn how to use your wizardly chill skills to create your own Winter Revels party. You can even make it "snow" inside!

Party Decorations

Why not make your own Crystal Cave for your Winter Revels? In some stories, Merlin is trapped in a cave made of shining, beautiful crystal. I've known Merlin for several hundred years, and he's a very clever fellow! So I have a feeling that if Merlin is living in a cave, it's because he wants to.

You can decorate your party room with your own version of the Northern Lights, the beautiful sheets of starlight in the sky over the North Pole. Tap tiny brad nails into the walls just under the ceiling, and drape loops of tiny white fairy lights, the kind you put on a Christmas tree, on the nails. Use masking or electrical tape to tape lights in place temporarily on the underside of tables and chairs for an unearthly glow (if electrical cords run where someone could trip, tape down the cords with duct tape for safety). Buy a few rolls of iridescent, see-through cellophane, the kind used to wrap gift baskets. Hang sheets of it from the walls for instant icy shine. While you're at it, wrap a few pieces of furniture so they're encased in make-believe ice! Add Magic Dancing Snowballs to the banquet table by following the directions on page 14 for the Dance of the Spheres Centerpiece.

Decorate a Frosty Wizard's Tree with more tiny lights and Soap Flake Snow (page 125), then hang the tree with Giant Icicles, Glittering Snowballs, and Perfect Snowflakes (page 126). One legend says it's because of our friend the spider that we decorate our holiday trees with icicles and tinsel. At the first Christmas in Bethlehem, some spiders were shooed away from a tree close to the holy manger. The spiders complained, and they were allowed to come back and decorate the tree with their webs, which the delighted Christ Child turned to silver.

Just for fun, see what the New Year will bring by "throwing the shoe." The Irish did this 300 years ago. Have each guest bring an old, worn-out shoe to the party (you might want to have a few extra on hand). Go outside and take turns throwing the shoes up and over the roof of the house. How did the shoe land? If it points away from the house, you'll take a trip in that direction. If it points toward the house, you won't be going anywhere. It's good luck if the shoe landed sole down, but if it landed upside down, you'll need to be extra careful to avoid mistakes or accidents. Don't like what the shoe says? Throw another one!

Snow Sorceress Robe

The young sorceress who wears this robe will shine brighter than the Ice Queen herself, and its faceted "ice" jewels will help transmit magical powers. If you can't find a polar bear to donate some fur to trim the robe, cotton batting or fake fur will do nicely. The key to creating a wintry effect is to use only icy colors and clear jewels.

WHAT YOU NEED

• Basic Robe on page 135, made with white or silver fabric
• 2 yards (1.8 m) of cotton batting or fake fur, 3- to 4-inch (7.6 to 10.2 cm) width
• straight pins or fabric basting spray
• white thread and sewing needle
• pattern on page 137
• pencil or chalk
• 1 to 1-1/2 yards (.9 to 1.35 m) of heavy-duty aluminum foil, silver polyester film, or fabric
• ball-point pen (optional)
• fabric adhesive
• spatula
• puff paint in silver and white
• microfine glitter in silver, white, and black
• clear plastic, faceted jewels, or "diamond" costume jewelry
• Crystal Crown on page 124 (optional)

INSTRUCTIONS

1. After making the Basic Robe, measure around the neckline, cuffs, and hem. Also measure the distance from the center front of the neckline down to the hem. Cut continuous strips of the cotton batting or fake fur to match the measurements; cut two pieces for the collar-to-hem measurement.

2. Use the pins or basting spray to attach the strips to the neckline, cuffs, and hem, and place the two neckline-to-hem pieces side-by-side down the front of the robe. Sew in place by hand or with a machine. Remove the pins.

3. Use a photocopier to enlarge the snowflake pattern on page 137 as desired. Cut out the pattern.

4. Trace the patterns on the mylar, foil, or fabric, and cut them out. If desired, use the blunt end of the ball-point pen to lightly emboss designs on the aluminum foil.

5. Using the spatula, spread a thin layer of the fabric adhesive on the back side of the cutouts, and smooth in place on the right side of the robe as shown. Let dry.

6. Lay the robe flat on a tabletop. Working only on the front of the robe, draw snowflakes, stars, or comets, and use the puff paint to outline the glued-on patterns. Add glitter, and while everything is still wet, add an extra dot of adhesive at key points and press on the "jewels." Let dry overnight.

7. Repeat step 6 to decorate the back of the robe.

8. Top your outfit with a Crystal Crown (page 124) if you like.

YOU'RE MAGNIFICENT!

Crystal Crown

Glinda, the Good Witch of the East, wore a glittering crystal crown that looked as if it was made of ice. (The munchkins and I thought it went very well with her gossamer gown.) You can make your own crown from silver poster board, fabric, or clear acetate. You can also use clear, ribbed plastic floor runner to give your crown the effect of finely cut crystal.

WHAT YOU NEED

- measuring tape
- calculator
- pencil
- ruler
- sheets of newspaper
- scissors
- drinking glass (optional)
- sheet of poster board, or 1 yard (.9 m) of clear acetate*, shiny fabric stiffened with iron-on interfacing, or clear plastic floor runner**
- cellophane tape
- tinsel rope, sequins, plastic jewels, metallic-colored acrylic paints, puff paints, glitter, and/or tinsel stems
- paintbrush (optional)
- white craft glue (optional)
- hot-glue gun and glue sticks (optional)
- hole punch
- round-head brass fasteners

*found on rolls in craft stores and blueprint shops

*the kind made for hardwood floors, not carpeted floors

INSTRUCTIONS

1. Use the measuring tape to measure the circumference of your head just above the ears. Add $1/2$ inch (1.3 cm) to that measurement. Using the calculator, multiply the total measurement by 4; then divide that number by 6.28.

2. Measure and mark a line (equal to the measurement you came up with in step 1) on the top edge of the sheet of newspaper. Start the line at a corner. Measure and mark a second line at a right angle to the first line down the side of the newspaper. Use the ruler or measuring tape to mark equal points from the corner.

Connect the points with a line forming an arc.

3. How tall should your crown be? Six to nine inches (15.2 to 22.9 cm) is a good height. Use the ruler and pencil to measure and mark the height you've chosen from the arc you just drew (figure 1).

4. Cut out the arc pattern you've just drawn.

5. Fold the arc in half and then in half again. This will give you a crown with four points. You can fold it in half, and then into thirds. A

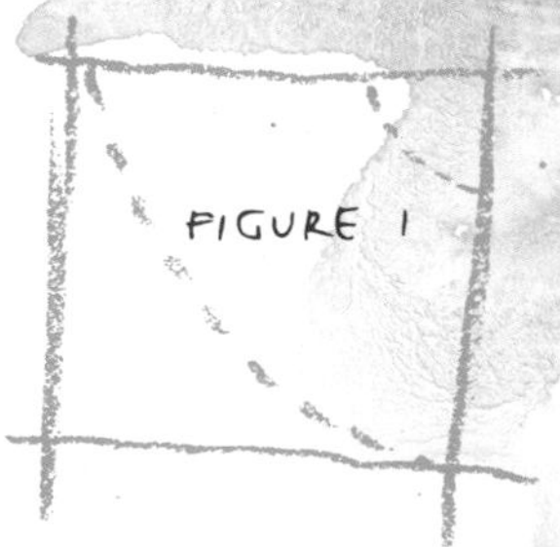

FIGURE 1

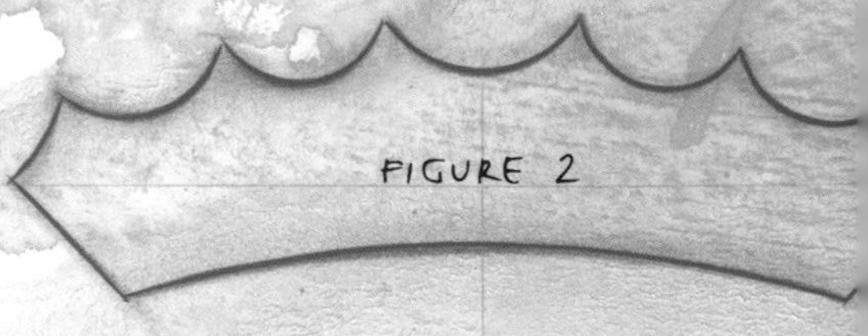

FIGURE 2

six-pointed crown is nice. Don't try to make too many folds or you'll find that your points become flat.

6. Use the pencil to trace the points on the folded paper. If you want a softer look, use a drinking glass as a template and draw arcs on the pattern. Cut out the pattern you've drawn, then unfold the paper (figure 2).

7. Place the pattern on your selected material. Use the tape to secure the pattern to the material. Cut out the crown.

8. Lay the crown on a flat surface and decorate it with anything sparkly, glittery, or shiny. Add accents with metallic paint, or cut out snowflakes (page 127) from silver paper to glue on the crown. Glue small sequins, beads, and jewels to the crown. Twist glittery tinsel stems into decorative shapes and attach them. Let any glued or painted decorations dry before you shape the crown.

9. Now you'll attach the two unfinished edges of the crown so it will stand up. Use the hole punch to make two holes on one edge. Overlap the edges of the crown a bit, and pencil in matching marks on the opposite edge. Punch holes at the marks. Use the round-head brass fasteners to join the two edges, or

Frosty Wizard's Tree
with Giant Icicles, Glittering Snowballs, and Perfect Snowflakes

Like magic, you can coat your Frosty Wizard's Tree with a heavy hoar frost and hang it with icy ornaments. Why stop there? Try hanging Giant Icicles from the ceiling too. They won't drip during your revels, and you can tell your friends you put a No-Melt Spell on them! Decorate a tree for your party room, and set out materials so your guests can make their own ornaments to take home.

WHAT YOU NEED (for the Tree)

- fallen tree limb, 3 to 4 feet long, with several small branches
- small bucket
- sand or gravel
- white craft glue
- disposable cups
- craft sticks
- granulated sugar
- talcum powder
- measuring cup
- small paintbrush
- spoon
- sifter
- transparent, white, or silver glitter (optional)
- quilt batting, tissue paper, or white cloth

INSTRUCTIONS

1. Before your party, take a walk on a winter's day and look for fallen branches. Don't cut a branch from a living tree, fairies hate that!

2. Place the branch in the bucket and anchor it with the sand, gravel or both.

3. Mix $^1/_4$ cup (2 fl oz, or 60 mL) or less of the white craft glue with an equal amount of water in the disposable cup, stirring it with a craft stick.

4. Mix $^1/_3$ cup (40 g) of the granulated sugar and an

equal amount of the talcum powder in a disposable cup.

5. Use the small paintbrush to spread the glue mixture on the branches.

6. Put a few spoonfuls of the sugar and talcum mixture in the sifter at a time. Sift the mixture on the branches. Coat the branches with more of the sugar and talcum mix if desired. The branches should glitter as if covered with a heavy frost. (If you don't want to make a sugar and talcum mixture, simply use the glitter in its place.)

7. Cut a length of the quilt batting or other white material and wrap it around the bucket to disguise it.

Giant Icicles

WHAT YOU NEED

• heavy foil oven liner
• ruler
• pencil
• scissors
• mandrels in different sizes, such as a wooden dowel, broom handle, and pencil
• sewing needle and white thread (optional)
• tape or thumbtacks (optional)

INSTRUCTIONS

1. Measure and cut long, even lengths of the oven liner. The width of the lengths can range anywhere from 1/4 inch (6 mm) to 3/4 inch (1.9 cm).

2. Wind a length of foil diagonally on the dowel, handle, or pencil. Make icicles of different diameters by winding them on the different mandrels.

3. You can make unique icicles with the following method. Hold one end of a length of foil with your thumb and forefinger. Place your other thumb and forefinger about 8 inches (20.3 cm) away and twist the section slowly. Watch for triangular folds to appear. Don't twist the foil after the folds appear. Move your fingers along the length and repeat until you have twisted the entire length.

4. Hang the icicles on the branch of a tree by folding over about 1/2 inch (1.3 cm) or less of one end of a length of foil.

5. If desired, you can cut, wind, and twist wider lengths of foil liner to hang from your ceiling. Thread a needle with a length of white thread, pierce one end of an icicle with the needle, and pull the thread through. Use the tape or tacks to hold the thread to the ceiling.

Glitter Snowballs

WHAT YOU NEED

• newspaper
• white craft glue
• disposable cup
• craft sticks
• transparent, white, or silver glitter
• foam meat trays or box lids
• paintbrush
• polystyrene foam balls of varied sizes
• waxed paper
• blow-dryer (optional)
• tinsel stems, cut into 2-inch (5 cm) lengths
• hot-glue gun and glue sticks

INSTRUCTIONS

1. Cover the work area with newspaper.
2. Mix some white craft glue with an equal amount of water in the disposable cup. Stir with a craft stick.

3. Pour the glitter into the foam tray or box lid.

4. Use the paintbrush to coat the foam balls, one at a time, with the craft glue mixture.

5. Roll each ball in the glitter. Set it aside on a

length of waxed paper to dry. If you're in a hurry, use the blow-dryer to speed the drying time. Be sure you use the low setting so you won't blow the balls away!

6. Take a tinsel stem and gently push it into a ball. Pull it out, then hot glue the stem in the hole you just made. Bend the end of the stem into a hook, and hang the snowball on the tree.

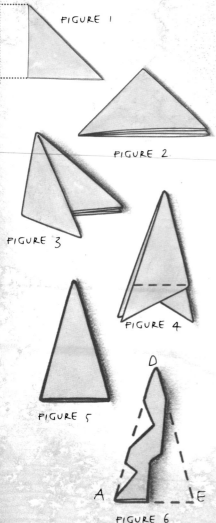

FIGURE 1

FIGURE 2

FIGURE 3

FIGURE 4

FIGURE 5

FIGURE 6

Making Perfect SNOWFLAKES

WHAT YOU NEED

• vellum, metallic, tissue, or printed papers

• scissors
• hole punch (optional)

INSTRUCTIONS

1. Practice makes perfect snowflakes. Your first ones may be a little off, but as you practice folding them, snowflakes will fly from your scissors in a blizzard! Start with a square of paper. To make your paper square, take one corner and fold it diagonally to the opposite side making a triangle (figure 1). Crease the fold with your fingernail or with the handle of the scissors. Trim the excess and set it aside. You can make tinier snowflakes with the excess.

2. Fold the triangle in half again (figure 2). Crease the folds as you did in step 1.

3. Here's the tricky part (and the secret to making perfect snowflakes). You'll now fold the triangle into thirds (see figures 3 and 4). The trick is to learn how to fold it equally before you crease it. Fold a point over and then fold the opposite point over. Fiddle with the fold until the parts fit nicely together, then crease the folds. After a few tries you won't even have to fiddle anymore, you'll just know how to do it without thinking about it—like casting a successful spell!

4. Use the scissors to trim the points that are sticking out (figure 5).

5. Now comes the fun part. Point A forms the six points of the snowflake and point D forms the center (figure 6). If you cut off D, you'll have a hole in the center. If you cut off E, the tips of your snowflake will have more points. Make cuts in the folded parts of the snowflake as desired.

6. If desired, use the hole punch to create small holes in the snowflake.

7. Unfold the snowflake.

NOW MAKE SOME MORE!

Gaming

Wizard's Top and Blizzard or Thaw Game

In the cold winter there is nothing finer (or funner!) than playing a round of Blizzard or Thaw? with a Wizard's Top. In this game everyone wins some and loses some, but it's all in fun. The shape of the top was inspired by the Icelandic wizard Freon's discovery that all snowflakes had six points.

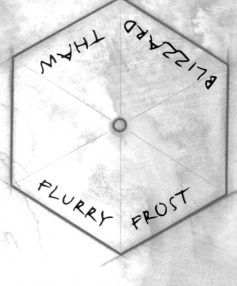

WHAT YOU NEED
(for the Wizard's Top)

- hexagon template
- scissors
- recycled plastic lid at least 4 inches (10.2 cm) wide, or polystyrene plate
- paint pens or permanent markers
- pencil
- plastic straw
- hot-glue gun and glue sticks (optional)

INSTRUCTIONS

1. Photocopy or trace the template. Enlarge it as needed.

2. Use the scissors to cut out the template pattern.

3. Center the template on the lid or plate and trace around it. Cut out the shape you traced.

4. Mark four sides of the shape with the words "blizzard," "thaw," "flurry," and "frost." For parties with other themes, use alchemical symbols, runes, or hieroglyphics.

5. After marking the center with the pencil, use the point of the scissors to open up a small hole.

6. Cut the plastic straw in half at an angle. Enlarge the hole you made and push the straw point first into the hole. The straw should fit snugly. If it doesn't, a dab of hot glue will hold it in place.

7. To spin the top, roll the straw between your hands and let the top drop.

Blizzard or Thaw Game

WHAT YOU NEED

• Wizard's Top marked with the words "blizzard," "thaw," "flurry," and "frost"
• small, wrapped hard candies or nuts (10 per player)
• basket or cup to serve as the "pot"

HOW TO PLAY

1. Each player should have an initial stake of candies or nuts to serve as markers. To decide who goes first, have each player spin the top. The player to spin "blizzard" goes first.

2. Before each spin, all players must put one marker into the "pot," which sits in the middle of the playing area.

3. Player one spins the top. If it lands on "frost," he gets nothing and must pass the top to the left. Everyone must put in a marker before the next spin.

4. If the next player spins "flurry," he gets to take half the pot before passing the top to the left. If the top lands on "blizzard," he takes all the pot and passes the top to the left.

5. If the top lands on "thaw," the player must put all of his markers into the pot, but he gets to spin again (whew!). If the top again lands on "thaw," he must pass the top to the left and wait his turn to spin again.

6. Keep playing for six rounds, in honor of the six points on a snowflake.

TELLING the FUTURE with TEA LEAVES

Several hundred years ago, some friendly Chinese sorcerers taught me how to predict the future by reading tea leaves. Simply look at the shapes the leaves form in the cup after you've drunk most of the tea. What do you see? Have party guests take turns telling each other's fortunes.

MARLA BAGGETTA

WHAT YOU NEED

• teapot*

ADULT WIZARD SUPERVISION!

• adult wizard
• loose tea leaves (you can use herbal mixes too)
• tea cups and saucers**

*You may want to prepare more than one pot at a time for your party.

**The cups should be wide at the rim, small at the base, and plain inside

INSTRUCTIONS

1. Set up a side table with chairs in the party room. Preheat the teapot by filling it with hot water from the tap. Put some water on the stove to boil (get an adult wizard's help with this). Empty the teapot and put 2 tablespoons (20g) of loose tea inside. Put the loose tea in the bottom of the pot so it can float around. Fill the teapot

with the boiling water. Set the teapot on the side table and let it steep
for
5 or 10 minutes.

2. With both of you sitting at the table, carefully pour the tea into a cup for
your friend. She should let it cool, then drink the tea. She must be careful to
leave a little liquid in the bottom so she can swirl the leaves around the inside
of the cup. The tea drinker swirls the leftover tea clockwise, around in the
cup, three times. (If she's right-handed, she uses her left hand to do this.)
She then turns the cup upside down and places it on the saucer.

3. Now you, the fortune-teller, pick up the cup and look at the forms created
by the tea leaves inside. The handle of the cup represents the tea drinker, and
any shapes stuck close to the handle affect her directly. The rim of the cup is
present time, and as the fortuneteller looks deeper into the cup, you're looking further into the tea drinker's future.

4. In general, distinct shapes mean the person is lucky. If the shapes are
unclear, she may have problems getting what she wants. Straight lines also
mean definite plans, while a rippled line means uncertainty. Numbers in the
top half of the cup represent hours or days, and numbers in the bottom half
stand for longer periods of time, up to years. Any letters are the initials of
people who will be important to her. There are many other symbols, and
some are listed below.

5. When you've finished reading the leaves, it's your turn to hear what your
friend sees in your future!

Balloon = troubles are ending
Bell = good news
Bird = good or bad news
Boat = travel
Book = wisdom
Castle = money!
Cat = a girlfriend is involved
Chair = a guest
Circle = frustration
Cloud = doubt
Clover = good luck!
Cross = bad luck!
Dog = a good friend
Elephant = a friend's advice
Flag = a warning
Flower = love and honor
Garden = prosperity
Gate = an opportunity
Heart = love
Horseshoe = good luck
Key = an opportunity, or discovery
of a secret
Knife = a misunderstanding
Man = a visitor
Scissors = an argument at home
Snake = an enemy
Square = protection
Star = success
Tree = a goal is successfully achieved
Triangle = good luck
Wheel = money

Yule Log Cake

ADULT WIZARD

SUPERVISION!

I always burn a Yule log to mark the passing of the winter season. But I think it's more fun to make one you can eat.

WHAT YOU NEED

- adult wizard
- chocolate cake mix, and the ingredients called for in the directions
- 17 x 12-inch (43.2 x 30.5 cm) jelly-roll pan
- aluminum foil
- butter
- flour
- 2 tablespoons (20 g) powdered cocoa
- clean dish towel
- 2 cups (.47 L) whipping cream, whipped until stiff
- spatula
- cake knife
- chocolate frosting
- fork

INSTRUCTIONS

1. With the help of an adult wizard, position the oven rack in the lower third of the oven. Preheat to 350°F (180°C).

2. Prepare the cake mix according to the directions on the box.

3. Line the bottom of the pan with the aluminum foil. Make sure there is enough overlap so the foil comes up over the edges of the pan and completely covers the inside.

4. Butter and flour the pan. Pour the batter in and spread evenly.

5. Bake the cake for 16 minutes, until it loses its sheen and springs back if pressed lightly. Dust the top of the cake with the cocoa.

6. Wet the clean dish towel and wring it out. Cover the cake with the towel and set it aside to cool.

7. When the cake is cool, remove the towel, grasp the edges of the foil, and gently slide the cake out of the pan. Place the cake on a flat surface.

8. Use the spatula to spread the whipping cream on top of the cake. Roll it up gently, using the aluminum foil for support, but don't forget to peel off the foil as you roll!

9. Refrigerate the roll for 1 hour. Cut a diagonal slice off one end and place it on top of the cake to form a knot in the log.

10. Spread the cake evenly with frosting. Use the fork to make bark lines in the frosting, then refrigerate the Yule Log for at least 1 hour before serving.

NORTH STAR COOKIES

If you make these cookies when the star Sirius (SEAR-EE-us), the planet Saturn, and the sun all appear in the sky at the same time, they'll float away! Luckily, this happens only once every six billion years.

WHAT YOU NEED

Yield: 5 dozen
- adult wizard
- large bowl
- medium bowl
- 1 cup (220 g) butter or margarine, softened
- 1 1/4 cups (250 grams) granulated sugar
- 1 teaspoon (5 mL) vanilla extract
- 2 teaspoons (3 g) grated lemon peel
- 1/4 teaspoon (1 g) salt
- 1 1/3 cups (185 g) flour
- 1 1/2 cups (340 g) ground walnuts
- plastic wrap

- star-shaped cookie cutter
- cookie sheets
- small bowl
- 2 cups (445 g) sifted confectioners' sugar
- 1 teaspoon (5 mL) vanilla extract
- 2¹/₂ tablespoons (37 mL) water
- wooden spoon
- food coloring (optional)

INSTRUCTIONS

1. With an adult wizard's help, pre-heat the oven to 375°F (190°C).

2. In the large bowl, cream the butter, sugar, and vanilla extract.

3. In the medium bowl, mix the lemon peel, salt, flour, and walnuts.

4. Add the flour mixture to the butter in several stages. Mix until well blended.

5. Use the plastic wrap to cover the dough and refrigerate for at least 2 hours.

6. Roll the chilled dough to a thickness of ¹/₈ inch (3 mm). Cut out cookies with the cookie cutter.

7. Place the cookies ¹/₂ inch (1.25 cm) apart on the (ungreased) cookie sheets. Bake for 8 to 10 minutes, until the cookies are golden brown. Let cool for 5 minutes.

8. Combine the confectioners' sugar, vanilla, and water in the small bowl,

stirring until well blended. Add additional water to the mixture if it's too thick. If you'd like your cookies to be colored (like a "red giant" star, perhaps), add a few drops of the food coloring to the icing.

9. Spread the icing over the cookies. Let cool, and store in an airtight container until serving.

HOT BUTTERED Not-Rum

Every time I accept an invitation to dinner at a castle, I end up sitting in a draft! A few sips of this drink warm me right up.

WHAT YOU NEED

- 2 tablespoons (30 g) unsalted butter for each wizard
- medium saucepan
- 1 cup (.24 L) apple cider for each wizard
- ladle

ADULT WIZARD

INSTRUCTIONS SUPERVISION!

1. Put 2 tablespoons (30 g) of butter in the bottom of each wizard's mug.

2. Pour the apple cider into the saucepan. Heat over medium high heat until just scalded.

3. Ladle the cider into each mug and serve.

The Snow QUEEN

Long ago, a wicked elf made a mirror that made good things look bad—and bad things look good. Blooming flowers looked dead in its reflection, and nice people looked mean and ugly. The elf flew high into the sky and dropped the mirror. Tiny pieces flew all over the world, scattering little bits of evil everywhere.

Just as the shards flew down, Kay and his best friend Gerda were out-side playing in the snow. Kay felt a terrible pain in his chest and his eye. The pain passed but the shards were in him, and Kay now hated everything he once loved. Good things looked ugly, and everything bad looked desir-able. He chased reindeer, made chil-dren cry, and started fights. He was even mean to Gerda. Soon everyone avoided him. One day, Kay stole a bicycle and rode it far out of town. It was dark and cold and scary. Remembering how warm and safe he used to feel at home, Kay started to cry and huddled under a tree.

Like magic, a glittering sleigh with a team of huge, snow-white dogs pulled up. A pale woman stepped out, dressed all in white with a halo of snow and shoes made of ice. She knelt down and hugged Kay, and he thought she was the loveliest woman in the world (remember, Kay could only see what was not). Kay had met the Snow Queen, who took helpless children to live with her at the North Pole. But she was so cold, her love slowly turned them all to ice. Kay couldn't even feel his own heart growing cold at her touch. She put Kay in the sled, and they rode away.

Meanwhile, Gerda was very worried. She went to talk to Kay to find out what was wrong. But when she got to his house, he was missing, and he had been so mean, even his own family members weren't sure they wanted him back!

Walking through the snow, Gerda met a little boy crying over his missing bike. Kay had stolen it, she realized, and started following its tracks. "What are you doing out here, all alone?" asked a voice out of the thin air. Gerda jumped, then realized a raven in a tree was talking. It kindly told her it had seen the Snow Queen take a boy away.

But how could Gerda reach the North Pole? She hitched a ride on a passing dogsled and rode to the Snow Queen's palace. It was huge, empty, and cold, lit only by the stars in the night sky. There was Kay, still and cold. His skin was almost black, and icicles dripped from his hair and fingers. Was he already dead? Gerda rushed to Kay, hugged him, and burst into tears. Her warm tears fell, melting Kay's frozen heart and dislodging

the evil mirror from his chest. Turning pink, Kay woke up. In tears from the pain of defrosting and his bad deeds, Kay cried so hard that the mirror shard popped right out of his eye! He was free. Once again, he could see good and bad things for what they really were. So Kay and Gerda went home, and remained friends forever.

Good Witches, Glamorous Goddesses, and Legendary Queens

AS TOLD BY THE WIZARD

Many of my good friends in the magical arts are women. I'm glad to see they're finally getting the attention they deserve! The Celts knew a lot about goddesses, who were strong and independent. Brighid (BREED) was a very important goddess. She healed hurt creatures and helped poets and artists with their work. Maybe the next time you make something wizardly, she'll give your project some extra power.

Most Celtic war goddesses didn't use weapons, because their looks and magic scared enemies. Legend says the battle cry of the Morrighan

(MORE-ee-ann), who was also called the Phantom Queen, was as loud as 10,000 men shouting. Men died from fear when they heard the goddess Nemhain (NEM-win) speak. Queen Medb (MAYVE) used magic to steal enemies' strength, leaving them too weak to win a fight. Scathach (SKEE-ach), known as "she who strikes fear," taught young Celtic warriors how to fight.

Do you have a cat at home? The beautiful Norse sorceress Freyja (FRAY-yuh) rode through the sky in a golden chariot pulled by black cats, and she wore a necklace that glittered as bright as the stars. (The King of the Dwarves made it for her.) Freya once turned her boyfriend into a large, golden pig so he could stay with her in the home of the gods. The Egyptian goddess Bast (BAAST) actually had the head of a cat! The Egyptians believed she helped the sun rise and set, and she was also their goddess of pleasure. You can see pictures of her on the walls of the pyramids.

Today, Italian children still look forward to a visit every January 6th from the good witch La Befana (LA bay-FAH-nah). She rides on a broom or a goat, and fills stockings with presents. Legend says she refused to help the three wise men during their trip to Bethlehem for the first Christmas. But now she travels the earth with a bag of gifts on her back and a lantern in her hand, forever looking for the wise men and the Christ child.

BASIC
Wizard Gear:

A MINI-MANUAL
FOR MAKING
A ROBE, WAND, STAFF, AND HAT

Parties are a very good excuse for making a hat or robe, and it's fun to show up at a party with something new. (I've noticed that a lot of nonwizard parents fuss about the same things before a big event: getting a new dress, washing the car, you know what I mean.) Anyway, you can adapt these instructions to match the theme of a party that you give or that you go to. On the other hand, you may also choose to wear your everyday robe to show you're a serious sort of wizard.

When you make your wizard things, don't be afraid to make choices that please you. I'm sure a sorceress was the first person to dare to wear red with pink, for example! And if you're fond of something, whether it's pigs or race cars, go

If you're serious about being a wizard, you really need a robe, a hat, a wand, and a staff for official business. These things also make it easier for other wizards to recognize you. Some of the tips I give in this book work better with the right utensils too. For example, magic potions have a lot more SHAZAAM! KAZAAM! KA-POW! when you wave a wand over them. In this part of the book, I'll tell you how to make all of these things.

ahead and put them on things like your wand (pigs can be magic; see my story about the sorceress Freya on page 133).

Finally, I share my number-one, most important secret for young wizards: the things you make yourself always have more power than anything you can buy at the store. (But it's o.k. for another wizard or a nonwizard, such as one of your parents to help you when you make things.) And the more fun you have making something, the more magic it contains. That's basic wizard secret number two. Finally, secret number three: a group of young wizards working together can often create new, fun things that just one wizard working alone wouldn't think of. That's why wizard parties are such good places to make magical items.

Basic Wizard's Robe

Have you ever peeked inside another wizard's closet? Some of us are secret clotheshorses! We have robes for every season, every party, and every kind of wizard work. This robe is very easy to make by hand or with a sewing machine. You can adapt the directions to make every single party robe in this book, or simply choose your favorite color and decorations. (I've always worn my purple and gold robe for really special occasions.)

WHAT YOU NEED

- measuring tape
- fabric yardage (see step 1)
- pencil, chalk, or other fabric marker
- straight pins
- scissors
- sewing needle and thread to match fabric
- sewing machine (optional)
- fusible hem tape or fabric glue (optional)
- bias tape
- 18 inches (46 cm) heavy cording
- photocopies of symbols in this book (optional)
- tracing paper
- water-soluble pen (optional)
- dressmaker's carbon paper (optional)
- large piece of cardboard
- fabric paint in colors of your choice
- paintbrush
- fusible webbing
- iron
- decorative trim, cording, or printed ribbon

INSTRUCTIONS

1. Ask a fellow wizard or sorceress to measure you with the tape measure to determine how much fabric you need. Stand with your arms down by your sides. Have your friend measure you from the top of your shoulder to the floor, then add 1 inch (2.5 cm) for the hem. Multiply this measurement by 2 to determine the cut length of fabric needed. Now have your friend measure you from one wrist to the other, across the back of your shoulders, and then add 2 inches (5 cm) for the sleeve hems. This measurement determines the width of the fabric you need. Fabrics 45 inches (114 cm) wide are usually wide enough for most wizards under the age of 10. Older wizards (or those with long arms) require wider fabrics or will need to sew on extra fabric for the sleeves. Now measure loosely around the base of the neck. Lastly, measure your inside arm length (from wrist to underarm), minus 2 inches (5 cm). Write all these measurements down for future reference.

2. Fold the length of fabric in half, right sides together. Lay the folded fabric flat on a large tabletop or the floor, smoothing out the wrinkles as you work. Pin the bottom edges together in several places.

3. Fold the fabric in half lengthwise (you will have four layers of fabric). Secure the open edges with a few straight pins. See figure 1.

4. Divide the total measurement from wrist to wrist, including the hem allowance, by 2. This measurement is the sleeve length. Measure and mark from the folded edge of the fabric to the sleeve length.

5. Determine how wide you want the sleeve of the gown to be; 12 to 15 inches (30.5 to 38 cm) wide should be fine. Use a pencil or chalk to make a parallel mark on the unfolded open side to the chosen measurement. From this mark, draw

a line equal to the inside arm length running parallel to the top fold (see figure 2).

6. Draw a line from the open edge at the bottom of the fabric to the mark for the inside arm length (see figure 3).

7. For the neckline, divide the neck measurement by 6. Measure and mark a point on the top and side folds from the folded corner. Connect the marks with a curved line to form an arc (see figure 4).

8. Cut through all the layers for the neckline and along the lines marked for the sleeve and sides (see figure 5).

9. Open up the robe and lay it flat. It will look like a T-shape, with the fold at the top.

10. Sew the side and sleeve seams with a $1/2$-inch (1.3 cm) seam allowance, by hand or by machine. Turn the robe right side out.

11. You can use fusible hem tape or fabric glue, if you don't want to sew the hems of the sleeves and the bottom of the robe.

12. Cut a 4-inch (10.2 cm) slit from the neckline down the center front of the robe (see figure 6).

13. To finish the edges, attach bias tape by machine or hand.

14. Use the heavy cording as a belt for the robe.

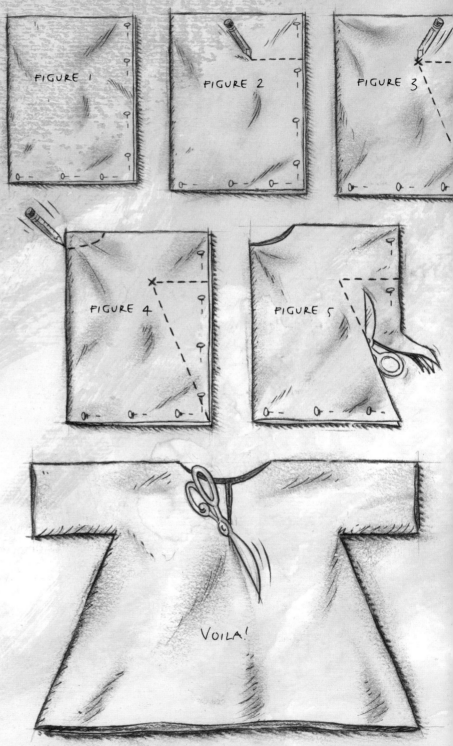

WIZARD'S ROBE 101

FIGURE 1

FIGURE 2

FIGURE 3

FIGURE 4

FIGURE 5

VOILA!

Decorating the Robe

1. First you will need to transfer the symbols you've chosen onto the fabric. There are several ways to do this.

• Tracing: The easiest way is to trace the symbols onto the fabric using a water-soluable pen or very sharp pencil. Simply draw or trace the symbols onto a piece of tracing paper and tape it to a window. Then tape the fabric on top and trace the pattern onto it.

• Dressmaker's carbon paper: This special fabric carbon comes in different colors so you can select one that clearly shows on your fabric. Draw, trace, or photocopy the pattern. Place the fabric on a clean, flat surface and tape it down with masking tape. Place the carbon paper face down on top, and tape it down. Use a ball-point pen to carefully trace over the pattern.

2. Use fabric paint to paint the symbols. (Of course, you can choose other designs. This is your robe.) Be sure to place the newspaper inside the robe before you paint on the fabric, or the paint will seep through both layers. Paint the neckline, sleeve, and bottom of the robe hems with strips or swirls of paint that look good with the painted-on symbols. Read the manufacturer's instructions that come with the fabric paint to find out how to heat set the colors using a hot iron. Ask an adult for help with this!

3. Enlarge the patterns on a copy machine. Use these patterns to cut out shapes from contrasting colors and textures of fabric. Attach the fabric shapes to the robe with fusible webbing.

4. Attach decorative trim, cording, or printed ribbon to the hem edges of the sleeves, neck, and bottom. You can do this either by stitching the trim in place or with fusible hem tape or fabric glue.

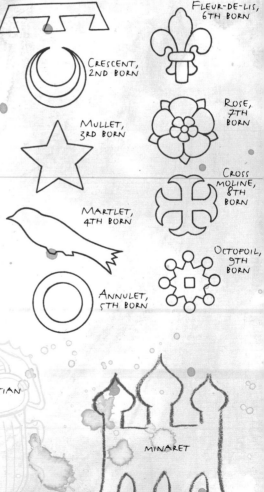

ALCHEMICAL SYMBOLS

CHINESE IDIOGRAMS

CADENCY SYMBOLS

FILE, 1ST BORN

FLEUR-DE-LIS, 6TH BORN

CRESCENT, 2ND BORN

ROSE, 7TH BORN

MULLET, 3RD BORN

CROSS MOLINE, 8TH BORN

MARTLET, 4TH BORN

OCTOPOIL, 9TH BORN

ANNULET, 5TH BORN

6-SIDED SNOW FLAKE

CELTIC SWIRL

EGYPTIAN HIEROGLYPHICS

SACRED EGYPTIAN SCARAB

MINARET

Basic Wand with Dragon Heartstrings

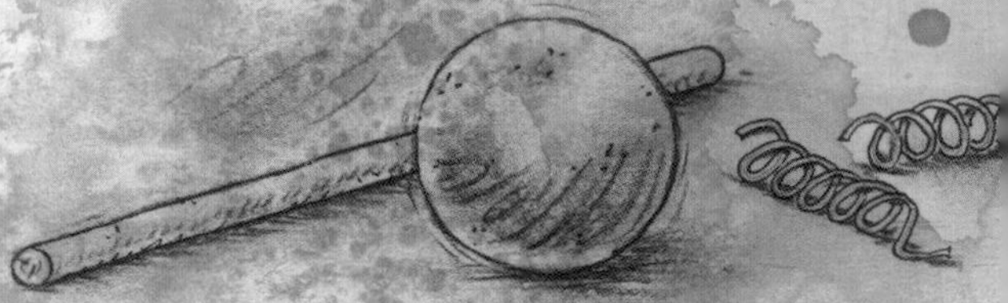

Any wizard worth his wand knows that dragon heartstring coils carry powerful magic, and some of us know how to make the strings of the heart go, "Zing!" Add several coils to your own wand to make it a stunner.

FIGURE 1

FIGURE 2

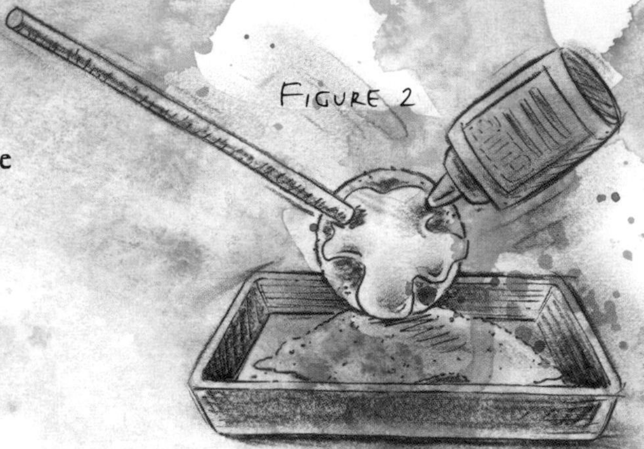

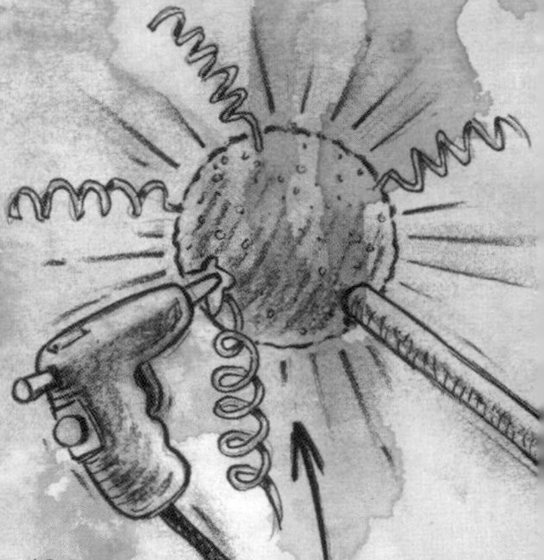

FIGURE 3

WHAT YOU NEED

- spool of brass or copper wire*
- ruler
- wire cutters
- pencil
- 2-inch (5 cm) polystyrene foam ball*
- gold, silver, or multicolored glitter
- white craft glue
- disposable plate or meat tray
- disposable paintbrush
- straight twig or wooden dowel, about 18 inches (45.7 cm) long and $1/2$ inch (1.3 cm) wide
- acrylic paint (gold or silver)
- paintbrush
- hot-glue gun and glue sticks

*sold in craft stores

INSTRUCTIONS

1. Measure and cut eight lengths of wire, each 18 inches (45.7 cm) long.

2. Tightly wind the wire around a pencil. Leave about 2 inches (5 cm) unwound. Repeat this process with the other seven lengths of wire (figure 1).

3. Lightly press the polystyrene foam ball onto the end of the stick so that it sinks down about 1 inch (2.5 cm) onto the stick.

4. Pour gold or silver glitter onto the plate. Using the disposable paint-brush, coat the ball with the white glue. Then roll it in the glitter to

coat it well (figure 2). Allow it to dry.

5. Use a clean paintbrush to paint the twig or dowel with gold or silver acrylic paint. Allow it to dry.

6. Use hot glue to attach the ball to the wand.

7. Put a dot of hot glue on the straight end of a wire coil, and insert the end into the foam ball (see figure 3). Repeat with the rest of the coils.

8. Make additional coils and insert them into the ball if desired.

Basic Wizard's Staff with Jeweled Orb

Kings often have royal scepters (SEPP-turs) topped with round balls called orbs—an idea they got from wizards, of course. The first king to do this thought the orb stood for the world (which he liked to think he ruled). But it was really just our way of keeping balls handy for a game of wizard bowls. That's where the term to "strike" with a staff came from (we never HIT anybody, for goodness' sake!). These days, we play at regular bowling alleys and our orbs stay on our staffs.

WHAT YOU NEED

- wooden closet rod, broomstick, or large fallen branch from a tree
- measuring tape
- pencil
- handsaw
- 8 feet (2.5 m) of small diameter rope*
- hot-glue gun and glue sticks
- acrylic paint in color of your choice
- paintbrush
- craft knife or scissors
- 6-inch (15 cm) polystyrene foam ball*
- table knife
- newspaper to cover work surface
- disposable plate or foam meat tray
- glitter
- white craft glue
- disposable paintbrush
- large plastic gems in a variety of shapes and colors

*sold in craft stores

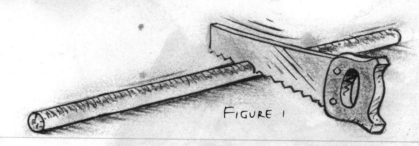

FIGURE 1

INSTRUCTIONS

1. The length of a wizard's staff should be in proportion to the wizard who will use it. A good rule of thumb is to make the staff 6 inches (15 cm) shorter than the wizard or sorceress. Measure and mark the staff material you have chosen.

2. Use a handsaw to cut off any extra length (figure 1).

3. Use hot glue to attach one end of the rope to the bottom of the staff.

4. Refer to figure 1. Wind the rope up the staff at an angle, gluing the rope to the staff about every 2 inches (5 cm). When you're about 2 inches (5 cm) from the other end of the staff, stop winding and gluing. Make sure you have about 10 inches (25 cm) of loose rope left (figure 2 on page 140).

5. Paint the staff, including the rope, and allow it to dry. Don't paint the last 2 inches (5 cm) at the top of the staff.

6. Use hot glue to attach the ornament to the top of the staff. Wind and glue the last bit of rope around the bottom of the staff ornament. If necessary, cut off the excess rope. Touch up this section of the staff with paint.

7. Center the polystyrene foam ball on the staff and gently push on it to make an indentation in the ball; then remove the ball. Use the table knife to hollow out a hole 1 inch (2.5 cm) deep and slightly smaller than the indentation.

8. Pour glitter on the disposable plate.

9. Paint the foam ball with a thin coat of white craft glue. Roll it in the glitter and allow it to dry for a few minutes (figure 3).

10. Use hot glue to attach the jewels to the ball.

11. Fill the hole with hot glue, and gently push the ball onto the basic staff (figure 4).

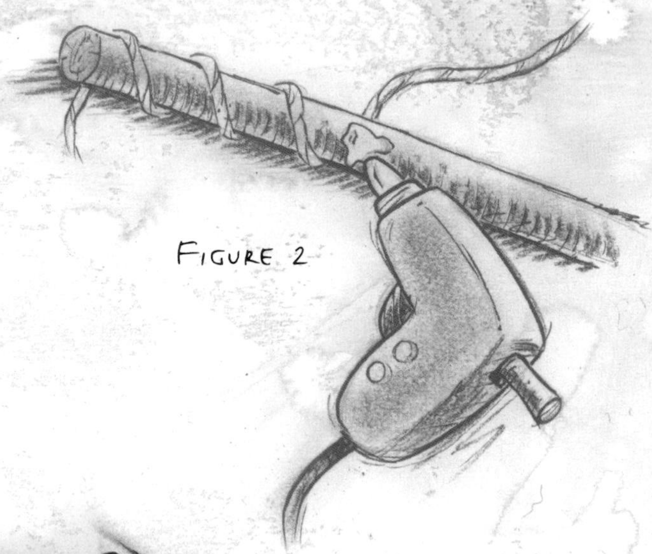

FIGURE 2

FIGURE 3

FIGURE 4

Basic Sorcerer's Hat

This hat is very easy to make, and it instantly tells people you're a wizard or sorceress when you wear it. (I mean, they can tell by looking at you, unless you've also put a Talking Charm on your hat. But make sure you know how to un-charm it! A chatty hat babbling nonstop in your ear can be most nerve-wracking.) You can make this hat in fabric that matches your robe, if you wish.

WHAT YOU NEED

- $1/2$ yard (45 cm) fabric or felt
- $1/2$ yard (45 cm) fusible interfacing (the stiffest kind)
- $3/4$-yard-wide (69 cm) wire-edge ribbon
- measuring tape
- pencil
- calculator
- sheet of newspaper
- ruler
- scissors
- straight pins
- fabric glue
- sewing machine or needle and thread*
- iron

FOR DECORATION (choose one or all):

- fabric scraps
- wide ribbon or braid
- metallic-colored acrylic paints
- paintbrush
- glitter
- rubber stamps

*Note: You don't have to sew this hat if you make it out of felt or paper. Simply use glue or an iron-on fabric adhesive to make the seam.

INSTRUCTIONS

1. Measure the circumference of your head (all the way around it) right above the ears with a measuring tape. Multiply that measurement by 4, then divide that number by 6.28. (Even wizards need to learn math!)

2. Measure and mark a line as long as what you came up with in step 1 (on the top edge of the sheet of newspaper). Measure and mark a second line at a right angle to the first line. Use a ruler or measuring tape to mark equal points from the right angle. Connect the points with a line forming an arc (see figure 1on page 142).

3. Use scissors to cut out the quarter-circle you just drew.

4. Place the pattern on your fabric. Pin the pattern to the fabric, and add a $1/2$-inch (1.3 cm) seam allowance to the straight edges of the pattern. Cut out the pattern.

5. If you wish to decorate your hat, do so before seaming it. Work on a flat surface. Decorate the fabric with stars, moons, or other symbols in this book. You can paint them free-

hand, or you can trace them.
Metallic-colored acrylic paints used
with rubber stamps and metallic gel
marking pens work too. Or cut out
shapes from gold or silver scraps of
fabric, and glue them to the cutout
hat (see figure 2).

FIGURE 1

6. Lay the decorated fabric on the
fusible interfacing. Cut around the
fabric. Follow the manufacturer's
instructions included with the interfacing that explains how to use an
iron to fuse it to the fabric (see figure
2).

7. Match the straight sides, right
sides together. Sew a $1/2$-inch (1.3
cm) seam along this edge by hand or
with a sewing machine.

8. Turn the hat right sides out.

9. You can decorate the rim of the
hat by stitching or gluing on decorative ribbon or braid. For a dressier
look, gather one end of a piece of
wire-edge ribbon and stitch it to the
back of the hat. Gather the ribbon
about 3 inches (7.5 cm) from this
end, stitch it to the hat, and repeat as
many times as needed around the
rim of the hat (see figure 3).

FIGURE 2

FIGURE 3

FAREWELL
from the Wizard

Sometimes the best time to say goodbye to your friends is in the middle of a grand party! If you've finished this book, you're probably ready to give your own wonderful, whizz-bang wizard's bash. So this is my farewell for now.

The whole point of a party (and a lot of life, I think) is to have fun and enjoy being alive. So be silly, play games, and show off your latest magic tricks and charms. (Just be sure you know how to reverse any spells you cast. It's very bad form to send a friend home as a toad.)

One more thing, and this is important. Our magic is always stronger when we gather together with friends and family. So why wait any longer to show them how special they are to you? Get your house elf to start writing those invitations now!

Oh, and by the way, when you plan the refreshments, add an extra cookie and a mug of cider or two.

JUST IN CASE I HAPPEN TO BE IN THE NEIGHBORHOOD.

Index

A NOTE ABOUT SUPPLIERS

Usually, the supplies you need for making the projects in Lark Books can be found at your local craft supply store, discount mart, home improvement center, or retail shop relevant to the topic of the book. Occasionally, however, you may need to buy materials or tools from specialty suppliers. In order to provide you with the most up-to-date information, we have created suppliers listings on our Web site, which we update on a regular basis. Visit us at www.larkbooks.com, click on "Craft Supply Sources," and then click on the relevant topic. You will find numerous companies listed with their Web address and/or mailing address and phone number.